THE TURN IN THE TRAIL

Northwoods Tales
of the Upper Great Lakes

THE TURN IN THE TRAIL
Northwoods Tales
of the Upper Great Lakes

WALT SANDBERG

Illustrations by Gordon Allen

WILLOW CREEK PRESS
Oshkosh, Wisconsin

Some of the stories in this book were previously published in slightly different form in the following publications: *Wisconsin Sportsman, Michigan Sportsman, Minnesota Sportsman, Trout, Fur–Fish–Game, Fins and Feathers, Midwest Outdoors* and *Outdoor Outlook.* I am grateful to the publishers of these publications for permission to reprint this material.

Library of Congress Catalog Card Number 79-91532
Published February 1980

Printed in the United States of America.
ISBN 0-932558-14-3

For those special people
who have traveled the turn
in the trail with me and
particularly for Carol, my wife,
and Lisa and Lori, my twin daughters

Contents

PART II

. . . to the upland fields and forests

PART III

. . . to Burnt Stump Lodge

EPILOGUE

Tribute

A log of birch is laid upon the hearth for warmth, a knot of apple wood for fragrance, and a handful of dried cherry twigs is cast into the flame to promote a sweet and lulling crackling.

It's midwinter, the time of year when those who love the outdoors sometimes turn away from the cold outside and from the windrowed snow and sweeping Arctic winds to sit, cradled in a favorite easy chair, reflecting inward on themselves about another year gone by.

"How went the year?" I ask my inner self.

"Not badly," it answers. "Trout fishing, if you recall, was a little slow. But that brace of smallmouth you enticed into chomping the white-feathered poppers on the Deerskin River in July made up for that."

I smile and nestle deeper into the softness of the chair while the soothing voice within my head chants on: "And the October day you walked into that migratory flight of woodcock . . . that was worth the week of days you spent in endless tramping with an empty gamebag slapping at your side."

"Indeed it was," I agree, vividly seeing, even now, the splash of autumn color across the hillside and those crazy-flying birds etching their spirited departures forever across my mind.

"Nor were the grouse unkind," the voice reminds me. "And those mallards coming off the beaver pond . . . you've never had such shooting."

"Yes," I answer, "it *was* a satisfying year."

"Don't be so smug," the voice disturbingly intones. "Haven't you forgotten something?"

"What's that?" I ask.

"Friendship. Hasn't it been a good year for that, too?"

"Indeed it has," I silently agree. "But I've not forgotten it."

And I have not. I really haven't.

Like most people, I am fortunate to have acquired a circle of acquaintances, several of whom, happily for me, have come to count me as a special friend. And for that I am thankful.

But sometimes, in those introspective moments before the crackling winter fire, I think: "What causes them to share their lives with me?"

Is it that they take me as I am, overlooking my many faults, praising only my desirable qualities?

I don't know.

But there is one thing that I have come to see: Each of them has something they do extraordinarily well. Perhaps that attribute envokes in them a high level of tolerance.

My friend Wayne Doucha, for example, is an exceptional food service manager and a master chef. He does his job so well that he has become a television personality. Thousands of erstwhile toast-burners watch his show on Sunday evenings just to see how the Master does it.

Then there is Ray "Gordy" Gordon, a cousin who is also a friend. Gordy is a woodsman of singular ability. If there is some work that needs doing in the North Country outdoors, Gordy can do it. Bulldozing roads, felling timber, slashing pulpwood, planting tree seedlings, building a nature trail . . . he is a Northwoods jack-of-all-trades and proficient at them all.

And my friend Paul Hoffman, an assistant collegiate football coach, is one of those persons so well attuned to his job that his vocation is also his avocation. Someday, I'm sure you'll see the Hoffman name in the headlines after coaching his Big Ten team to victory in the Rose Bowl.

And there are many more, those special people who do things well and call me friend: Ed Matuczak, tire salesman; Wayne Armstrong, engineering technician; Terry Kroll, soil scientist; Danny Kroll, a truck painter who can take a packet of seeds or a handful of dried roots and turn them into acres of glorious flowers and succulent vegetables; Don Sandberg, distinguished purveyor of cemetery plots and mortuary slots; George Schussler, three-hundred-sixty pounds of affable bartender; Bus Grove, biology professor and university dean; Bill Hilts, over-the-hill hockey player; and Frank Coffey, symbiotic learning specialist (whatever that means).

They do things well.

Still, they're ordinary people. If you were to meet them on the street you would probably pass them by as being of no importance. And you would be the loser, as I would be if, by circumstance, I had never come to know them. For by merely seeing them, you cannot recognize the passion and the talent that they possess inside.

One thing else distinguishes these special people: each enjoys hunting and fishing and camping and has an innate and unusual sensitivity toward outdoor things.

Each loves the woods, the fields, the hills, the animals. They are at harmony with nature and thereby with each other.

Ed Matuczak can spot the slight dimple of a rising fish a quarter-mile upstream in the roaringest of trout water.

Bus Grove can overturn a streamside rock and tell you, by examining the churned-up mud, what kind of fish are in the stream, what they eat, and the biological history of the entire area.

Gordy can look at a pine tree and tell you what part of a backwoods cabin it will make.

Wayne Doucha can rustle up a gourmet dinner from mushrooms and watercress and a haunch of squirrel.

Maybe that is why we are such special friends. Although widely separated by age, experience, geography and technical ability, we have, whenever we get together, a common sympathy—a love of the great Northwoods outdoors.

Perhaps one of those special friends is escaping winter tonight by reading these words before a warming fire of birch and applewood and cherry twigs.

And if they've read this far, they might be saying, "My friend, you wrote that well."

And if they have . . . if they have overlooked my many shortcomings to admire work that I do, sometimes well, it is another tribute to their friendship.

PART I

. . . to the lake, river and stream

Moonrise on the Avedon

*L*et me take you where you've never been before. Let me take you to the Avedon.

I've fished it often when the misty twilight rolls through the pinetops and the probing fingers of the moon search its silent hidden valley.

I know it, although I do not know it well. Not many do; it's hard to find. The Avedon is a mysterious and secluded trout stream which feeds life into the headwaters of the wild Popple River beyond the reach of many anglers.

Few today can even remember its lilting name, taken from an immigrant Scottish family that lost its dreams along the Avedon's infertile, rock-strewn banks a generation or more ago.

Today, painstakingly built remnants of that futility still remain: tiny meadows hand-hewn from the virgin forest, outlines of squat fieldstone fencerows now hidden under encroaching trees, a family burial plot, and the memory of a lilac.

What backbreaking labor must have created this place. What hopes must have inspired the builders. How dreadful it must have been to cull a field of stone each spring to make way for a crop which, at best, would be too sparse to feed a hardy family.

And how painful it must have been to finally realize the inhospitable nature of this land and to give it up with family buried in it.

I crossed the homestead to reach my favorite trout lie on the Avedon. And to get there I passed a lilac bush that lived tenaciously in the corner of their meadow.

Each spring it greeted me with fragrant purple blossoms and I reflected: "What joy the blooms must have given Mrs. Avedon after the hard, drab winter."

For it was she who had planted the lilac bush, of course. Mr. Avedon, the crusty old Scot, would not have catered to such

[3]

frivolity—at planting time he would have had more pressing things to do . . . like picking rock.

To get to the trout I must pass a tombstone in the corner of their shrinking meadow. The stone, inscribed with the surname Avedon, marks the resting place of Bryan and Shiela, the immigrants who shared their lives with this isolated soil.

So today, their struggle can be re-created by all who wander here. It's recorded in the purple lilac, in the shrinking meadows, and in the fieldstone fencerows that once pointed my way to the best fishing on the Avedon.

To get to the good fishing, at an extraordinary trout hide that I call Bryan's Bend, I mark my route by Shiela Avedon's lilac bush then turn to travel Bryan's fencerow north. The last stones are dribbled to the streambank and form a rustic armchair which can comfortably accommodate the laziest of anglers. Bryan himself, I think, must have sat upon this same stone chair, after church, to take a Sunday dinner of native brook trout for the Avedon clan.

Some might say that it is not right that I remember the Avedon's harsh and unrewarding history while in the search for pleasure. I don't know.

But, I reason, they won't begrudge me for it—so little pleasure they must have had themselves.

I think that's true.

I *know* that's true.

For once, at moonrise, in early spring, when Shiela's lilac was fairly bursting forth with joy, I sat upon the stony chair and thought I heard a whispering from the forest. "Fish the Lilac Pool," it said. "Fish at Bryan's Bend . . . in the moonlight."

And I thought I detected, too, the rolling of a Scottish brogue in that whispering of the wind.

I fished the Lilac Pool, of course, for like most anglers I believe in omens.

But I did not take a fish that night.

The next spring, when I again walked the Avedon in search of the huge brown trout that rose there only in the evening, I plucked, for some unknown reason, a sprig of purple lilac and sought to find the Avedon's remains.

The tombstone was hard to find. I knew it was in the aspen clone at the northeast corner of their dwindling meadow, but this year the opening was smaller—Nature had invaded.

Still, after trodding back and forth, I found the stone. It was choked with newly emerged creeping nettle, wrapped with baby burdock, and tendriled with freshly sprouted hazelnut brush.

I tromped the vegetation down as best I could until the earth before the stone was almost smooth. And gently, with unaccustomed reverence, I placed the lilac sprig.

Then, light-hearted, I went fishing, at Bryan's Bend, on Lilac Pool.

That night I fished before the moonrise bathed the Avedon, transforming it into a mystic, fairy-tale stream. The valley was cobalt black with the shadows of evening and I heard trout smacking insects from the underside of the pool. But none rose to my fly.

Then, just as I was about to quit this most pleasant of pastimes I heard, again, that now-familiar whispering from the trees:

"Fish where the moonlight parts the water," the whisper said.

"Where the moonlight parts the water?"

I cast my fly, a huge, showy White Miller, precisely at the interface of shadow and moonlight.

And I took a fish. Then another! And several more.

It was the most unbelievable trout fishing I've ever had. It was ecstasy. On every cast a trout . . . *if* I dropped the fly accurately at the interface.

Yet if I placed my fly too deeply into the shadows, I would have no strike. Nor could I entice a fish if an errant cast curled the fly too far into the moonlight.

But when I dropped it at the interface, precisely at interface, I always hooked a trout and it was always a good one.

I had fun that spring, fishing in the moonlight, on the Avedon, at Bryan's Bend, on Lilac Pool. And I shall remember it always.

I *have* to remember how it was. For Shiela Avedon's lilac, with its fragrant purple blossoms that herald spring, and Bryan Avedon's streamside fishing chair, are no more. They were cleared away last summer to make room for a widely advertised plat of vacation homesites. Insightfully, the developer's advertising agency has chosen to call it "Whispering Valley."

The Avedon is still there, of course. And so is the tombstone.

But the lilac bush is gone . . . bulldozed under for Lot 17.

Still, I often visit Lilac Pool and Bryan's Bend at twilight, when the moonlight anoints my holy waters.

[5]

But it's not the same.

I no longer have the desire to cast a fly at Bryan's Bend now that the banks are denuded and the quarry is hatchery-raised.

And I no longer hear the whispering from the forest in that distinctive Scottish brogue, nor can I gather a sprig of purple lilac in the spring to honor Shiela Avedon.

That last perhaps, is what saddens me most of all.

A Kinship with the Past

*E*ach Opening Day of trout season, as warm rains promote the spring runoff on my favorite Northwoods stream, I find evidence that earth does not wish to hoard reminders of the past but annually unburdens itself of them.

In turn, the regurgitated relics arouse the curiosity of the fisherman and he stoops to retrieve these springtime offerings as keepsakes of a day pleasantly spent.

Near Willow Pool, the best early-season trout hide on the river, an icy torrent has uncovered a rusty cone-topped beer can. The shape identifies it as being about thirty years old—evidence of an angler with litterbugging habits of the generation before my own.

A few long and unproductive casts upstream, near Redhorse bend, the winter wind has undermined a gnarled cedar tree that toppled in the first spring thundershower. Clutched in its exposed roots is the oxidized iron head of a logger's stamp. It was used nearly a century ago to mark ownership of the white pine logs which were rafted to downstream markets in the spring.

Beyond the cedar, where a jumbled buttress of pewter-colored boulders is receiving its annual repolishing by the rushing water, the obelisk of granite that I am standing on to add distance to my cast suddenly totters. And as it falls I see beneath it, wedged in other smaller stones, the remains of a trade tomahawk—part of a cargo lost when a French voyageur's canoe swamped here late in the seventeenth century.

But the most cherished find this day is a pair of arrowheads—one of exquisitely fluted chert, another of hammered copper, now corroded green. They have been sorted from the bottom gravel by the natural action of a swirling eddy in the backwash of Camp One Rapids Pool.

The first arrowhead, to my layman's eye, appears to be a Folsom Point the style and workmanship of which can be attributed to the

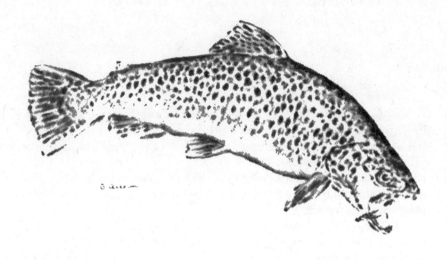

earliest inhabitants of the Great Lakes Basin.

The second arrowhead is more easily classified—it is a remnant of the Old Copper Culture Indians who flourished here long before the time of Christ.

I am exhilarated at finding them. For in these artifacts I have acquired a direct tie with the people who roamed this river valley one thousand . . . two thousand . . . eight thousand years ago.

So powerful is the legacy of these relics that when I touch them I can actually feel the influence of their makers surge through the objects to fill me with a magical feeling of awareness. At that moment, I have the sensation that I am living at the time of these ancient artisans.

Strangely, I can even clearly understand the thoughts of my arrowheads' creators. And it is pleasant to find that their concerns are not unlike my own: the worry for food, shelter and love, the need for a sense of purpose, and an awe of the unknown.

Then suddenly, I see the arrowheads for what they truly are: sort of cosmic amplifiers.

The arrowhead makers are the transmitters. I am, by virtue of being here, the receiver. The communication medium is the atmosphere of this place. And the arrowheads, when touched, draw from this historic river valley the faded impulses of the past and intensify them, much as a tuning fork pulls invisible and inaudible reverberations from the air to transform them into discernible sound.

Although that may be true . . . it's also highly unlikely.

A more plausible explanation for my strange experience at Camp One Rapids Pool might be that I've recently read a book about North American archaeology and I'm now misinterpreting my recent acquaintance with prehistory as a cerebral link with ancient man.

I have learned, for example, that man probably entered the New World from China, about twenty-seven thousand years ago. His access road was a land "bridge" over the Bering Sea which connected the Chukchi Peninsula of Siberia and the Seward Peninsula of North America during the Ice Age. Later, as the glaciers melted, the bridge flooded and remains impassable.

The first people to cross were a band of hunters in search of game. Paleo-Indians we call them today. Others followed.

Some bands, we know, wandered leisurely southward at a pace of about four miles a year. Eventually they reached the Great Plains which were lush and profuse with game.

Then, somewhat more than eight thousand years ago, descendants of the first Americans roamed from the plains to the shores of Lake Superior, settling on what is now the Bayfield Peninsula.

There they created the Red Paint and Old Copper Cultures, imaginative outposts of civilization that influenced the world of the time out of all proportion to their numbers.

And now, thousands of years later, I am holding pieces of this heritage in my hands.

So my earlier sensations, I decide, are illusory and will momentarily spend themselves in reality. The arrowheads are not sublime amplifiers but merely wedges of mineral and stone that once were chipped and hammered into a more useful form. Inside, the atoms of copper and chert are arrayed in precisely the same manner as in the unworked natural materials found nearby. The arrowheads possess no inherent cosmic force. They have not been sanctified. They are inanimate.

Contented now that I have explained the mystifying feeling that had overwhelmed me earlier, I lay a small cooking fire to butter-fry the native brook trout that I have creeled for my supper.

[9]

My fireplace is the same ring of rocks I used when I first fished Camp One Rapids Pool some twenty years before.

Absently, as I wait for the flame to rise, I scrape at the mound of charcoal and ashes which has built up and spilled from between the rocks after all these years. "How long," I muse, prompted perhaps by the events of the day, "have campers used this fire ring?"

Soon I have scratched a thin trench several inches deep. And when my casual scraping has increased the depth to about a foot, I can see that the layered charcoal extends deeper still.

I notice, too, now that the fire is higher, that the particles of dust which float airborne from my digging are being reburned in the leaping flames. Some glow bright blue—others orange, green and a dreamy shade of fluorescent pink.

Then, for a moment, I imagine that I see in them the effigy of an arrowhead maker toiling on this very spot millennia ago.

I peer intently at the ghostly form, hoping to ascribe to it some pattern, when I feel again that strange sensation of kinship with the past. And for the second time that day I am filled with an eerie sense of timelessness and historic continuity.

Only then do I chance to look down into my hand at the instrument I've used to scrape away the ashes of a thousand yesterdays. It is the Folsom Point.

The Pool Beyond the Willows

*B*ig Ed emerged slowly from the tangle of streamside alder brush—wet, weary, scratched, mosquito-bitten, fishless, and dejected.

"Bad day?" I inquired.

"You know it!" he replied.

We'd been friends for a long, long time, Big Ed and I. Even as the years wore on, bringing kids, bills, and class reunions—mileage hard to overcome—we would manage at least one fishing trip together every other trout season or so. And always when we'd meet again—eight months, a year, two seasons later—it was as if no time had passed at all.

One thing else had never changed between us. Big Ed was a jovial character who enjoyed putting people on. His pranks were always underplayed and never malicious, but jokes no less. And whenever we bantered together I always came out on the short end of it.

But today I *knew* I had him!

"Why not try upstream where that long pool tails out just beyond the willows?" I asked. "This time of day the shadow of that leaning tree on the east bank points directly to a midstream rock. And behind that you'll find a trophy brown."

Big Ed laughed.

"You sound pretty sure of that trout," he said. "Precisely how far do you predict its nose will be from the backwash of that boulder? A foot? A yard?"

"Since I've caught and released him several times," I lied, "I suggest you try whipping one of your atrociously tied muddlers exactly 7.5 centimeters downstream of the third bubble."

"Do you guarantee a strike?" Big Ed scoffed.

"I can with this donation to your cause," I said.

He caught the plump, squirming nightcrawler in midair, laughed again, and dropped the wiggling creature into an empty cigarette package and that into a pocket of his tattered fishing vest. Then he turned to squish back upstream, his leaky waders spurting tiny rivulets of tannin-dyed water at every step.

"Careful you don't spook him," I called. "You sound like a broken-down irrigation pump. He'll hear you coming from a mile away."

Big Ed saluted my advice with a slight dip of his rod, held high to wiggle through the brushy maze he'd fallen out of so ungracefully only moments before. As the tunnel closed behind him he snagged his boot on a twisted root and went crashing to the water's edge below.

I chuckled to myself and muttered to the sounds of struggle: "If that isn't a typical Big Ed exit I don't know what is."

Then, in anticipation of Big Ed's unwilling but certain return, I rooted out a huge, curved chunk of burnt pine stump and balanced it against a white cedar blowdown. It would make a comfortable backrest to nap upon and to dream of how good it would be when I finally stuck Big Ed.

Three fat, speckled beauties rested in the cooling sweet fern in my creel. That was enough. For Big Ed didn't know I had them. And after sending him off on a midmorning fishing trip to nowhere, I deserved a quiet doze indeed.

The music from the rapids soon dulled my senses to the world outside and, contented now, I nestled down in the musty, leafy remnants of a year gone by to savor the pleasure yet to come.

For there was no pool beyond the willows, no midstream rock, no monster brown trout lurking just beyond. Big Ed would never find the fishing hole to which I'd so graciously directed him because it never was.

No trophy brown would ever slash that erstwhile angler's ineptly thrown morsel anywhere in this stretch of river. This was brook trout water, so cold the oldest native was seldom more than ten inches long. No polluting species of warmwater trout had ever been planted here. We'd see who the joker was in this operation. One thing for sure—it wasn't to be me.

Then suddenly, as I dozed so peacefully, there was a powerful shaking at my shoulder. It wrenched me from my pleasant reveries of revenge.

Faintly at first, then welling louder in my sleep-dazed mind, I heard a breathless voice exclaim: "He was just where you said he'd be—downstream of that big rock off the tip of the willow's shadow. Came right out of the water to take my streamer on the first cast . . . before it even hit the surface . . . two feet long if he's an inch. But I lost him!"

"Of course," I taunted. "There surely was a fish. Two feet long you say?"

And without opening an eye I rolled to plump the dusty pine root into a better pillow with a few smacks of my hand. Then I curled back to sleep in the warmth of a near-noon sun.

Months later, when I trudged that same stretch of stream while chasing grouse from swamp to covert, something—a quiet, gnawing doubt perhaps—held me from wandering too far from the riverbank, looking for the pool beyond the willows and a monster trout nearly two feet long.

Predictably, I saw none, although it was spawning time and any trout that size should be easily spotted working over the shallow gravel riffles.

Why I ventured there, I'll never know. For the pool beyond the willows is, of course, a pool that never was—it's as non-existent as Big Ed's monster trout.

. . . Perhaps.

Sauerkraut Trout

Charlie was a trout. A loveable, sag-bellied, old brown with a hooked underjaw that gave him the appearance of having a perpetual smile. He had a playful personality, too, which reminded us of a certain tuna of television commercial fame and in recognition of whom our Charlie had received his name.

But Charlie the Trout was craftier than his cartoon counterpart and until the day Hillard Selvey discovered his single weakness, Charlie also had a reputation for being uncatchable.

Hillard and I, among others, had tried to catch Charlie, unsuccessfully, for more than three seasons. Each of us hooked him several times but Charlie always managed to get away.

Indeed, it seemed as if Charlie deliberately attacked whatever bait we threw at him, aware that his strength and cleverness could foil any angler. Many of his hapless victims, including me, swore that Charlie relished spitting our hooks so that he could taunt us afterwards with a disdainful flip of his tail. It was a case of a fish having deftly played the fisherman, rather than the other way around.

Wisely, Charlie chose to live in a place that promised to protect his reputation. His home was a deep hole under a sandy cutbank beneath the roots of a huge white oak whose branches spanned the South Branch of the Oconto River off Highway 32 north of the village of Suring. The overhanging branches made casting impractical. And the roots prevented hardware and dry fly fishermen from placing lures close enough to Charlie's lie to tempt him into striking.

Occasionally, a minnow or a nightcrawler, properly weighted and dangled into the current upstream of the roots would get through the snaggle. Charlie simply stripped the offerings from the hooks and smacked his lips.

But heavy-hackled, weighted streamers—the more garish the better—often worked well. Using sinking-tip fly line and a delicate

[14]

tapered leader, they could be fished through the obstructions where Charlie would gleefully pluck them away.

"That trout," Hillard said once, "must be trying to stock his own tackle shop."

"You tell 'em, Hillard," we replied, for Hillard Selvey was a master of the art of streamer fishing and his flybook had yielded a good portion of Charlie's growing collection.

Hillard, too, knew the wiles of the South Branch as well as anyone. He fished it every chance he got—whenever he could get away from the always-pressing duties at his nearby farm.

Hillard's place—now more than seven hundred acres—was one of the largest and most prosperous farms in Oconto County. He had inherited the buildings and one hundred sixty acres from his immigrant parents, added land whenever he could afford more, and with a combination of hard work, luck and brilliant business acumen built it into a productive showcase.

So I wasn't surprised when Hillard announced that he had finally taken old Charlie, since he went about everything he did with calculated presistence.

"Six pounds, fourteen ounces," he said as he flopped the carcass on the bar in Mertz's Tavern. "And you owe me a steak dinner."

"Don't worry, I'll pay off," I said, "How'd you take him?"

"Sauerkraut juice."

"Hillard," I said, "I thought you gave up cussin'."

"No, you heard right . . . sauerkraut juice," he repeated. "He's a *German* brown trout, ain't he? And all Germans like sauerkraut. So I figured he could be coaxed into swallowing a streamer if it was disguised with kraut. It worked! First, I chummed some of the kraut into the river upstream of his hold. Then I doused a Number 2 Tinseled Maribou Muddler with the juice. He inhaled that juiced-up muddler faster than a wino sucks gin. Didn't even notice I was using twelve-pound mono for a leader."

"My God," I said, excited by the news. "Do you realize what you have here? It's a trout fisherman's dream. A sure-fire killer lure! If it caught Charlie, it should catch every big brown in the river."

"Exactly," Hillard said, keeping his voice low. "So let's keep this between ourselves. I'm telling you about it only because you help me with the haying which, incidentally, comes up again in about two weeks."

In the days that followed I couldn't concentrate at work, anticipating the trophy trout I'd wrestle from the South Branch now that I was party to the secret that had finally bagged old Charlie.

Eagerly, I awaited my next day off and after taking care of some chores at home, I was on the road to the South Branch by midmorning. My first stop was the village store in Suring.

"Where's the sauerkraut?"

"Sold out," the matronly proprietress said. "Nine cases in the past week. That's more than I usually sell in six months. I can't understand it. Maybe the Ladies Guild is circulating a new recipe."

It was getting late and I didn't want to make the twenty mile round trip to Gillett, the next town of any size on Highway 32, just to pick up a can of sauerkraut. So I parked my car in Mertz's lot and tried my luck with streamers and dry flies, creeling three eating-sized brown before the sun went down and turned the superheated sky into black gauze over the river.

Mertz's beer sign, of course, was a welcome sight after the heat of the afternoon and I slid onto a stool to take care of my thirst.

"Draft?" Mertz asked.

I nodded.

Down the bar, two other patrons, both dressed in the forest green uniforms of the State Department of Natural Resources, sipped orange sodas and talked intently between themselves.

"The test results just have to be wrong," one of the men was saying. "There isn't a sauerkraut factory within fifty miles of here."

"I don't care if there isn't," the other said firmly. "Those water samples we took yesterday show a high concentration of sauerkraut juice. I'll stake my reputation on it."

I laughed, momentarily choked on my beer, and spewed a mouthful over the bar. The two men turned and looked at me strangely.

"What's the matter?" Mertz hastened to wipe up the mess.

"Hillard . . ." I replied. "That wily old buzzard did us in. A good share of his farm is planted in cabbage!"

[16]

The Sweetest Music

Once, in New York City, I heard the incomparable violinist Heifetz draw from his resined strings Tchaikovsky's Concerto in D. It was beautiful. I can hear the sweetness of the music still.

And once, in Kyoto, Japan, the oriental magic of the samisen prelude to a kabuki drama subdued my senses. The memory of that performance lingers, also, in the resonance of my mind.

Every once in a while, too, my body involuntarily sways to the still-remembered rhythms of Mariachi Vargas De Tecalitcan playing in the village square of Mazatlan, Mexico.

And sometimes, from the South Sea island of Tahiti, I can still recall the mesmerizing chant of a hundred brown-skinned beauties undulating their lithe and winsome bodies in time with an ancient litany so old none can recall its origins.

I hear all that. And I enjoy. Yet, as background to those sensuous and memorable sounds, I hear still more—I hear the sweetest music. Nothing can drown it out. No man-created orchestration can ever capture its timbre and sonority.

It is the rollicking melody of water cascading over Camp One Rapids in the spring to swirl merrily through the pool below.

And downstream, the slower, wider river sets up a cadence that is more restrained but no less forceful. The waters swish and purl and gurgle, carving the underwater trout hides and washing thousands of waiting brook trout free from their rocky winter environment. A year from now, if I am fortunate, a few will find their way into my creel.

To accompany this aqueous harmony, like the rumble of kettle drums resounding across a concert hall, is the sound of a ruffed grouse booming on his chosen log at mating time.

Boom!
Boom-Boom!
Boom-Boom-Boom!

[17]

Boom-Boom-Boom-Boom-Boom-Boom!

Then a momentary pause . . .

. . . And *Boom-Boom-Boom!* again, rising in intensity until it's a crescendo that leaves echoes rolling through the forest to reverberate forever in my mind.

No rock group can ever hope to match the power of that majestic sound.

In the forest, too, away from Camp One Rapids Pool, where the sound of rushing water is little more than a muted sluicing, the springtime angler hears another captivating natural symphony as he approaches a secluded beaver pond.

The frogs are here, hundreds of them, each voicing its happiness at having escaped the dormancy of a mud-encapsulated winter home to live in the splendor of a reawakened world.

One May, when the ruffed grouse boomed here and there in the distance, and the frogs croaked in unconducted unison in the nearby beaver pond, I put my ear close to the bud of an aspen tree as the morning sun touched its silvered twig. And I actually heard a leaf unfurl. At first it squeaked. Then it made a minor popping sound. And after that it fairly banged into life, the pale green leaflets grabbing for the sun.

Occasionally, too, I sit near the tail of Camp One Rapids Pool listening to the *slurp-slurp-slurp* of feeding brook trout working in the shallows, the cymbal-crash of a beaver's tail against the surface of the pool, and the muffled chuckling of a mallard family dunking for snails among the cattail.

When, several years ago, I chose to get to Camp One Rapids Pool by hiking in over the uplands rather than by battling the current upstream by canoe, I found that the fallen leaves of autumn no longer crunched underfoot but squished instead.

So sometimes, now, I make my own spring music simply by walking here. Usually, I make a waltz—two steps forward, *squish, squish,* and two steps back, *squish, squish.*

And when I take those two steps back I see something that in my haste I have missed before. At the base of an oak tree, neatly camouflaged, a hen grouse incubating next Thanksgiving's dinner.

She has laid one egg each day in May until she had a clutch of fifteen in her nest. Thereafter, I know, she won't leave it unattended unless the nest is directly disturbed, which is unlikely, because for reasons still not understood she exudes little scent this time of year.

[18]

Indeed, a well-trained hunting dog can nuzzle within inches of a nesting grouse without discovering its favorite quarry.

Another silent and scentless creature in the spring is the white-tail fawn. If you happen to walk upon one in the emerging undergrowth, consider yourself extremely lucky. For some primal, inborn quality directs this dainty, spotted woodland youngster to stay put, except when summoned by its mother. Not even a winter-hungry coyote, I am told, can detect the presence of a bedded white-tail fawn.

Yes, I still hear often, spilling from the subliminal recesses of my mind, the sounds of Heifetz, the chanting of the islanders, and the samisens and Mariachis. And I enjoy.

But I hear daily, welling up within me at the oddest moments, the waters of Camp One Rapids Pool surging merrily with spring, the booming of the ruffed grouse rolling through the forest, the syncopation of the frogs, and the delightful smacking of the feeding trout. It is the sweetest music.

A Golden Morning

Golden-bottomed Willow Creek was low and slow, sluggish in the midday heat of late July. Days before, the hatches of giant Green Drakes had passed their season's apogee and now the Willow was barren of insect life—devoid, it appeared, even of trout.

Still, I flayed the surface of Sandy Run almost daily with particular attention to the backwash of a certain midstream boulder that split the current rounding an ellipsoidal sandbar thrusting from the deepest part of the run. The polished chunk of granite shielded, too, a tiny coldwater spring which bubbled from the bottom there—the favorite feeding station of a tremendous hook-jawed brook trout.

Once I'd seen the fish roll. Another time I saw it evanesce a great *cecropia* moth which happened to struggle near it. And although I'd never hooked this lordly fish, I aimed to—even if it took all season.

As I cast to probe the water around the rock with my fly, quite certain that I would not raise the trout this time of day under these conditions, I caught a flutter of movement on the streambank in the periphery of my vision.

It was a young belted kingfisher, feathered out enough to fly, but now grounded, perhaps from lack of food.

I rummaged for the worm box which I always carried while astream, but kept hidden in an inside pocket of my fishing vest should I inadvertently encounter some purist acquaintance.

Popping open the box, I selected a medium-sized nightcrawler and dangled it before the bird. Its mouth snapped open, its jaws locked, neck extended, and the youngster began to emit pitiful gurgling sounds. I slid the tail of the worm into the bird's throat and it engorged the offering in three long and salacious gulps. Then it weakly squawked for more. Two larger nightcrawlers later, the bird fluffed its feathers, apparently content, and nestled down to sleep in the cup of my hand. Since I couldn't leave it in the open where some wander-

[20]

ing predator might select it for a snack, I gathered some dried marsh grass and made a nest in my wicker creel. Gently, I set the bird inside the creel and picked up my rod to pursue the trout. Later, when the bird had recovered enough to fly, I'd release it near the desiccated spire of a drowned tamarack which it might find suitable as a feeding perch.

"Thank you," a gentle and melodious voice seemed to whisper from the creel. Confused, I glanced into the access hole.

"No, silly," the voice said pleasantly. "Over here."

I glanced about and there, on the sand bar, lay a most gorgeous creature. Her waist-length golden hair was burnished with tones of bronze and copper that flitted about wherever the sunlight struck. Her grey-green eyes, the color of birch leaflets in the spring, had depths that slid away forever. Her skin glowed, too, as if lit from a powerful light within. She was utterly lovely. And she was naked.

"Excuse me," I sputtered, embarrassed. "I didn't know you were here. I . . . I . . . don't mean to intrude on your ah . . . sunbathing. I'll leave . . ."

The golden creature smiled. "Thank you," she repeated, "for saving me."

"Saving you?"

"Yes. I was the bird. What do you call it? A kingfisher?"

I looked into my creel. The bird was gone!

"When I'm in other worlds," she explained, "I take the form that suits me."

"Ah," I said, "the form you have now is perfectly agreeable to me."

She laughed. "I'm happy to see that you're no longer embarrassed by my form. On Xanthous no one is ever embarrassed by any form we choose to take."

"Xanthous?"

"Yes. My world is Xanthous. It's in the third galaxy beyond the universe your world is in." She stretched languidly and rolled on the hard golden sand. There were dimples on either side of her coccyx. The effect was charming. And I became, shall we say, agitated?

"I arrived only today," she said. "I was sent here by my government to entertain the most powerful creatures in your world so that we might become better friends."

"I'm for that," I admitted.

She smiled. "I am . . . how you say . . . an emissary? Yes. An

[21]

emissary. I travel to all the inhabited planets in your universe so that our governments might become friends, so that we might form an alliance against the people of the dark."

"The people of the dark?"

"Yes. They are bad people . . . From the world of Yeorbis, in the Fourth Galaxy, Second Universe, Ninth Dimension. They wish to engulf us all."

"You said you were the bird."

She laughed. "I made a mistake. When I arrived I saw all the kingfishers and thought they were the most powerful creatures on your planet. The baby kingfisher's mother had just dived into the water of the stream and speared a minnow fish with her feeding beak. I didn't know that there were other, more powerful creatures on your world, so I took the form of the young kingfisher, hoping that in its misery the kingfisher government would have compassion on me and hear my words."

"Then you saw me."

"Yes. And I saw you were more powerful than the kingfisher bird and that you fed it and had compassion so I changed to your form."

"Ah . . . not exactly."

"Sex is one thing Xathonians may not alter, whatever form we take."

"Thank goodness," I said.

"What?"

"Thank goodness you're here," I said. "We've had much turmoil on earth lately."

"Earth?"

"Yes. That's what this world is called."

"What a lovely sound . . . Earth . . . so much more simple to say than Xanthous."

"What is your name?" I asked.

"Name?"

"Yes. What do they call you on . . . on Xanthous?"

"On Xanthous they call me *eich* . . . *twine* . . . *none* . . . *zone* . . . *frei.*"

"What?"

"In your language it would mean 3627-Phi. But you may call me Patra."

"Patra?"

"Yes. Patra. It means precious . . . no . . . it means the *color* of precious metal."

"Patra," I said, "you are indeed that. You are indeed the color of precious metal. Welcome to Earth. I am called 399–30–0133."

"Earthlings are digitally identified, too? I will feel at home."

"It's getting that way," said I. "The number I gave you is my social security identification. I must list it on every paper nowadays. But you may call me Walt."

"Walt? What does that mean."

"A lover of creatures who are the color of precious metal."

Patra laughed. And the sound twinkled, harmonizing with the bubbling waters of Sandy Run. It was a moment of magic.

"Walt . . ." she called, beckoning to me from the midstream sandbar. "Come to my side so that I might know you better."

The water between me and her was well over my wader tops. I *knew* that. Still I plunged in. Whereupon I slipped. And my waders, filling with water, ballooned, dragging me down. Finally, I struggled to the sandbar.

As I surfaced, Patra laughed. "You earth people can change forms, too. Before you were skinny; now you are fat."

I waddled out of the run on all fours, squished my way to the summit of the sandbar, rolled over, lifted my feet, and the water poured out of the waders over my head, where it was instantly blotted up by the golden sands.

"You are . . . how you say it? Drenched." Patra said. "You must undress. I will dry you with my golden hair. Then I will give you a sonic massage to relax your muscles."

"A sonic massage?"

"Yes. I do it with my eyes. The high frequency waves from my eyes can excite the flesh." She reached toward me with an exquisitely shaped hand. Her fingers were long and supple, perfectly formed.

I put my hand in hers. The mere touching was sensual. She drew me to her.

And then, in the periphery of my vision, I saw it! I saw a rise! The swirls were swept downstream from the bubbles of the spring in the backwash of the boulder but it *was* a rise!

I dropped Patra's hand and reached, instead, for my fly rod. I began my false cast even before I was fully upright. If this was the brook trout I'd been after all these weeks, I aimed to get it now.

"Whatever are you doing?"

"Quiet!" I said. "Your noise will put him down."

"Whatever are you talking about?"

"The trout. The brook trout. I've been after him for weeks and I shall have him."

"You tricked me," Patra said.

"Tricked you?"

"Yes," said Patra. "You allowed me to believe that earth creatures in your form are the most powerful among you. Now I see that you are not. This . . . this trout . . . this *brook* trout obviously is more powerful than you."

"How's that?" I inquired, absently, intent on letting out just enough line to drop my fly to the right of the boulder where the current would take it, without the hint of drag, into the window of the feeding trout.

"If your form was the most powerful," I vaguely heard Patra's admonition over the swish of my fly line, "you would not be so intent upon capturing that slim and lovely creature who lives in these waters. You would be more intent on me . . . the emissary from Xanthous. It's quite apparent that the creature you seek to destroy is the most powerful being in your Earth-World, otherwise you would not have dropped my hand to pursue it. I must warn them. I must warn these brook trout. For they must surely be more powerful than you."

I scarcely heard, for by now my line was extended enough to delicately drop the fly precisely into the eddy of the current near the rock. And I knew that if I allowed the tippit to curl softly down, I would have my trophy.

As I lifted my arm for the final cast, I heard a splashing sound behind me. I turned my head. Patra was gone. The riseform of my brook trout had vanished, too.

I cast once more, but I could not raise the trout. I cast again, to no avail.

The brook trout did not rise that day, nor did it rise the next day, nor the next.

Indeed, I've never again seen a fish of any kind, not even a chub, feeding behind that boulder in Sandy Run where the bottom of Willow Creek is the color of precious metal—the color of Patra of Xanthous—the color of a golden morning.

Comet Creek Special

*H*erb Lemke was known as the best flyfisherman in north-central Wisconsin, a state that has less than perfect credentials as a purist's paradise—he *always* took trout.

But Herb had a peculiarity, too. He preferred fishing wet flies to dry.

Even when an unusually prolific hatch dappled the surface of the largest pool, or in midsummer when the waters of Shawano County's Red River were low, slow, and transparent as moonlight—dry fly only weather—he elected to fish wets.

"Why use wet flies when the hatch is on?" I asked one calm, humid evening as we strung our rods on the banks of summer-lazy Comet Creek, a feeder stream to his favorite Red River.

"Because they always take fish," he replied.

"What pattern will you be using tonight?" I probed.

"I'll try my Comet Creek Special," he said, not offering to show me what his special was. "But any wet will do. Trout aren't as finicky as most fishermen make 'em out to be . . . It's the presentation that's important."

I chuckled at Herb's reply, for it was always the same. The only variation he ever made in it was to preface the word "special" with the name of the particular stream we would fish that day. Herb had a North Branch Special, a Brandywine Creek Special, a Flume Creek Special, even a Mill Pond Special, and dozens more. He had wet flies for each of the waters he regularly fished, or so he said; for none who fished with him had ever seen any of them, only the results.

"Aren't you carrying the art of selective trouting a little too far?" I once asked.

"Not when the method takes fish every time out," he said with a slow grin. "I'm not one who fights success."

That evening on the Comet, after we had finished the ritual of

streamside tackle assembly and paused before entering the stream to admire a high, clean sky mellowed with scudding clouds of lemon and pink, Herb casually waved an index finger upstream, then down, indicating that I should take my choice of water.

"You go up tonight," I shook my head. "I took it first the last time."

Ordinarily I would have welcomed the advantage, for the half mile upstream boasted the best fishing on the Comet.

But tonight I wanted Herb to have this select stretch of trout water all to himself so that I might complete the scheme that had rolled into my mind one fishless day several weeks before. I would follow Herb along the gnarled course of the Comet and quietly watch his technique from deep within the screening bankside brush. Perhaps that way I might discover what his skillful presentation had that my artless one did not. And if I could indeed find out how he did it, the lost fishing time, precious though it was, should prove well spent.

We entered the stream together, Herb slowly moving upstream and I swiftly down. As I rounded the first bend where my exit wouldn't be detected from above, I put up my rod, stripped off the cumbersome waders, and slipped into the rubber-soled deck shoes I'd cached in my creel before leaving home. Then, humming to myself in anticipation, I carefully moved upstream along a path rutted deep by generations of fishermen. A spongy layer of thick moss and sodden leaves muffled the sound of my footsteps. Herb wouldn't hear me until it was too late.

Suddenly, as I neared the small clearing where we had parked the car, a faint, metallic squeak signaled caution.

Was someone at the car? Out to steal the camera perhaps? Or maybe the binoculars? Several anglers had recently reported losing gear in the area.

I peered beneath the tangled stems of alder brush and saw a wader-encased body shoulder-deep into the truck.

It was Herb!

He had a habit of forgetfulness and, inevitably, whenever we fished together, he would need to quit the stream within moments of entering it to retrieve some essential piece of gear. Still, something inexplicable held me lurking in ambush, watching, waiting.

Finally Herb glanced fitfully about, his body still partially hidden in the trunk, and then withdrew something that momentarily flashed dull silver in the rays of a steep afternoon sun. Whatever it was quickly found its way into the front pouch of Herb's waders. The object's shape was strangely familiar, but I couldn't see it clearly and its purpose escaped me for a moment.

Then suddenly I knew! And laughing I burst from my brushy hiding place.

"Lemke!" I cried. "I've finally got you! Wait till the boys hear this . . . Wisconsin's greatest flyfisherman caught with a wading *minnow* bucket. No wonder you say that you always fish wets."

Later, Herb grinned as he explained that most large trout he had observed seem to prefer their food alive and in big chunks. "Minnows are the largest share of a trophy trout's diet," he explained. "Flies and other tiny critters might appeal to a large trout as an appetizer or as dessert, but not as the main course."

"Yes," I laughed, "and you, I suppose, aren't really a traitor to the art of flyfishing. You're just a sort of piscatorial Robin Hood who robs rich minnow ponds to give the poor fish what they want . . . then hides the unsavory details from his buddies."

"Precisely," Herb agreed. ". . . they wouldn't understand."

"That," I said, "is a lousy job of rationalizing. Doc Faye won't buy it. Neither will Big Ed."

"Doc Faye!" Herb sputtered. "That hypocrite has been dunking worms on the sly for years. Did you know *that?*"

I admitted that I didn't and much less couldn't believe it.

So Herb quickly bribed me into silence by splitting his minnow supply—thin, silver darters only three-quarters of an inch long—and by plopping a half dozen tiny, shankless bait hooks into my outstretched palm.

"Don't use split shot," he cautioned. "Just let the minnow drift and sink naturally."

That evening, using Herb's special "wet fly," and by following his advice on proper presentation, I took several good trout from the waters of the Comet, some from holes that had always proven barren before.

Although Herb died several years ago, I still vividly recall that summer evening on the Comet.

In the intervening years his exploits as north-central Wisconsin's best flyfisherman have grown to become near-legendary—for I've never before told the story of his wading minnow bucket.

And every now and then, when I venture streamside with someone who knew him, it casts me in good light when they sometimes grudgingly admit that I've become almost as fine a trouter as his remembered reputation says he was.

"You always fish wet flies exclusively, too," my companions will generally observe, "just like he did."

And then they probe, as I once did with Herb. "What pattern will you be using tonight?"

"I think I'll try my special," I reply, properly prefacing the word with the name of the particular stream we will fish that day.

But I never show them what it is.

Brothers in Spirit

Angus Loonsfoot—my "native American brother"—struggled into the flickering light from our campfire and dumped a huge pine stump on the woodpile.

"What's that for?" I asked.

"To make the bonfire," said Angus, "for the trout dance."

"The trout dance? I've never heard you mention that ritual before."

"It's new to the tribe. I invented it this morning after we got skunked."

"I suppose anything is worth a try," I said, for we had fished the river hard for two days without raising a trout. Last season, the same stretch of stream—Class I trout water—had yielded several good-sized fish.

"The dance will work all right," said Angus confidently. "Didn't I make it rain last year?"

"Yes," I admitted, then reminded him: "But you made it rain in November . . . for deer season. It was supposed to be snow."

"Well," he shrugged, "sometimes these things go awry. An extra stomp of the foot, a slight deviation in the chant, and you get a variation in results. I'm a little rusty at this stuff, you know."

Angus Loonsfoot was a member of the Bad River band of Ojibways and his heritage spanned thousands of years. His great-grandfather was a Scottish fur trader who had settled in the area before the territory had become a state. Angus had learned the ways of the North Country from his grandfather, who had lived well into his eighties, and from his father, whom everyone calls the best woodsman in the area.

Angus, who holds a Bachelor of Science degree in limnology—the study of fresh water ecosystems—works for the state department of natural resources. Whenever fish and game refuse to conform to biological principles, he puts his cultural background to use in pursuing them. That the old ways occasionally appear to work, when science said they shouldn't, was reason enough to continue to believe in them.

Now Angus rolled the stump into the fire. The hot coals, touching the pitch, soon engulfed the resinous wood in flame. The fire crackled and sputtered, leaping ever higher, rising toward the night.

"*Sou-eee!*" he called, beginning a shuffling dance around the roaring fire.

"I think you've got something screwed up, Angus," I said. "That wail sounded more like an Arkansas hog call."

"There's some Natchez blood on my mother's side," said Angus. "The Natchez spirits must have taken over."

"The only Southern spirits in you," I said dryly, "come from a bottle of Jack Daniels."

"*Sou-eee!*" Angus responded.

Far off in the night a wailing cry echoed his call. The sound started low, increased in intensity, then trailed off when it reached its highest note.

"You sure you're doing a trout dance? That sounds like a coyote to me."

"I told you I invented the dance only this morning. It will take a while to perfect."

Then Angus pulled me from my seat on the camp stool and I imitated his shuffling dance around the fire.

"*Sou-eee!*" I croaked, self-consciously at first, then louder, with abandon.

The coyote calls rose to match our enthusiasm. And we danced faster and faster, howling back at them.

Finally we tired and slumped down near the fire, wheezing and gasping. "I thought your people accepted whatever nature gives you," I said. "But here we are trying to con the Water God into giving up its trout."

"Not true," said Angus. "Indians weren't the conservators of natural resources that the shamans of today's ecology movement would have people believe they were. The Indian was no worse and no better than other cultures when dealing with nature. We're all brothers in spirit in that respect. My ancestors took whatever they could, whenever they could. When they cleaned the game out of one area, they moved on and cleaned out another. That's how we became the first Americans . . . Oh, no, we're not *native* Americans, just the

[30]

first Americans . . . We came here from China, following the game, looking for greener pastures. Left on our own, without European interference, we would undoubtedly have multiplied and messed up the world as badly as you Whiteys did."

"*Sou-eee!*" I said.

"Right on," said Angus, continuing on what certainly seemed to be his favorite subject. "This myth of the sanctified Indian being at one with nature in the Golden Age of Mankind is what's responsible for the sad condition of my people today. We think we shall somehow revert to the Glory Days of our past . . . By always dreaming of how things were, we've lost our adaptability as a people. That attitude will be responsible for the extinction of my race; I aim to change it."

"But look how the early whites exploited you," I said. ". . . Trading the island of Manhattan for a case of beads and swapping valuable beaver pelts for cheap hunting knives."

"In the context of history," Angus explained, "my forebears thought it was the other way around. In those days skins and pelts held little value for the Indian. Nor did land. We thought we were exploiting you whites when we traded land and skins for glass beads. At the time, the beads had higher value. You see, the Indian made the same mistakes that the early white settlers did. Both believed that the land and the beaver would never run out."

"If that's the case," I said, "why the sudden rush for reparations? Why are today's Indians insisting that they be paid for land they traded away hundreds of years ago?"

"Show me a court suit by an Indian tribe asking for compensation and I'll show you a slick attorney behind it working on a contingency fee. Those guys are pandering to my people. They're instilling a something-for-nothing attitude. Why should an Indian work to better his condition when there's a promise that we'll all be rich tomorrow? It's destroying our integrity. The whole idea is absurd?"

"How's that?"

"Look at it this way," said Angus. "If I sold a house five years ago for $25,000 and, because of inflation, it can be resold today for $45,000, am I, as the previous owner, entitled to receive the $20,000 profit? Of course not! And neither is the Indian entitled to the difference between the value of the beads he received a hundred years ago and the current value of the land.

"But that's what the attorneys say we're entitled to," Angus continued, "and they know that you guilt-ridden Whiteys will pay off. Now let's get back to dancing up some trout."

As we rose to continue the trout dance, a high-pitched voice, emanating from the night like an untuned duck call, ended our ritual: "Trooper Hayes, here," the voice squeaked. "Just what are you Injuns up to? You're disturbing the peace. The other campers are complaining."

The glint of a silver badge and the shine off the blue steel of a massive revolver preceded the trooper's huge body into the light. "You ain't Injun," he said.

"No, sir, sheriff."

"I said *Trooper* Hayes," he reported. "I ain't the sheriff. Now tell me what all this hootin' and hollerin' is about. And what you say better be to my liking or you'll be doing your carrying on from a cell hall."

"It's a trout dance," said Angus, explaining how we'd been skunked and that we were willing to try anything to put the fish back on feed.

Trooper Hayes smiled and holstered his revolver. "I know the feeling," he said. "I'm a trout fisherman myself. But you boys can dance from now to sun-up and it won't do you a bit of good, not on this stretch of water."

"Oh? We've done well here in past seasons."

"Last October," Trooper Hayes related sadly, "a farmer upstream of here accidentally drained a tank of herbicide on his cornfield and it washed into the river. The stuff killed every living thing from there clear down to Bruce Crossing. It'll be years before the trout come back."

"*Sou-eee!*" Angus wailed.

Far away in the night a chorus of coyotes took up the call; from this distance it sounded very much as if they were crying.

[32]

Just Plain Fishin'

Time was when I would row my dad to his favorite offshore weedbed in a leaky $3-a-day rental boat to leisurely fish for Lake Michigan perch. Occasionally we took sagging stringers. Sometimes we didn't get a nibble. But we always had fun.

In those days the only technique I had mastered was bobber fishing. So my tackle was something less than that which is displayed in the fishing catalogs today.

I used a hollow steel extension rod of unknown brand, a balky level-wind bait-casting reel of unknown vintage, and a frayed, braided cotton line of unknown strength. This make-do assembly culminated in a rusty hook held on by a simple overhand knot—the only kind I knew how to tie—which usually unravelled after a few minutes underwater.

The bait was always a redworm hastily spaded from the low spot in the garden on those rare Sunday afternoons when the Old Man declared, "Boy, it's about time we do some fishin'."

Today, whenever I think about fishing with that outfit, I somehow feel guilty. For sometime between then and now I've acquired the notion that if I'm not fast trolling, back trolling, structure fishing, spoon plugging, jigging or popping, I shouldn't be catching fish nor having any fun.

So I don't go just plain fishin' anymore. Instead, I go streamer fishing, dry-fly fishing, ultra-light spinning, wire-lining, or downrigger trolling.

And to get to that weedbed I once paddled to, I hire a charter boat complete with U.S. Coast Guard licensed skipper and a first mate—at $60-plus for the half-day.

The fee, I reason, is well worth it. The charter arrangement provides me with boat, experienced guides, gear, and a scanning sonar to locate the fish.

Once the fish are found, the mate selects the lure, ties it to the

leader with a proper knot, and trails it at the proper speed and depth. Then he seats me in a cushioned reclining swivel chair and allows me to nap until a fish strikes. The moment it does he gently wakes me and shows me how to reel in my trophy before netting it, cleaning it, and arranging to have it smoked whole or fileted and flash-frozen, according to my wishes.

Affluent fishing, of course, is what I dreamed about while bailing that leaky rowboat those many years ago. And it is, indeed, a privilege of my modest success which makes the wistful boy still lurking within me feel extremely good.

But somehow, now that I've the money and the leisure to spend several days each year assuaging my youthful fantasies, the experience isn't what I envisioned it would be.

I recall, for example, when my palms fairly sweated just thinking about uncasing, at streamside, a Tonkin cane flyrod built by Leonard, Payne or Orvis. Even better to contemplate was fishing with a level-wind casting reel that wouldn't backlash merely by raising the rod tip.

But now that I've had the chance to use the latest tackle to fish in those exotic places that I once located by patiently searching the *Hammond World Atlas*, fishing no longer seems the pleasure it used to be.

Some days I even feel like vowing: "To hell with all this fancy gear . . . I'm going back to just plain fishin'."

But now that I've become an outdoor writer of at least peninsular acclaim, I don't and probably won't. What would the readers say?

More important, what will my editors say? If I don't supply them with a flow of material about new hotspots, sizzling techniques that will fill the live box every time out, or news of innovations in tackle that will entice fish into attacking whether or not the moon is right or the feeding urge strikes, they won't buy and I won't eat.

Still, I long to return to those languid Sunday afternoons of bobber fishing on Lake Michigan. The huge corks allowed an unwary fish to strike and then suspended it until we got around to horsing it in. Looking back, it seems to me that in those days we controlled the fish and by so doing we also controlled the fishing.

But today, using the sophisticated tackle the experts tell me I must use if I'm to have fun fishing, things appear to be the other way around. The fish are controlling me and therefore also control my fishing.

I'm told, for example, that a responsible angler should fish a trout stream only with dry flies. But dry-fly fishing and me don't coordinate too well. The technique requires an instantaneous response. And I don't have it. I always strike too early or too late.

When I strike too early, the line rockets from the water and tangles in the brush behind. When I strike too late the fish spits the hook and flashes off to its next downstream lie. And I, conditioned in the alleged purity of this deceptive sport, trudge wearily off to intercept it, although I know full well that the attempt will only result in a repeat performance.

Late last season, I decided that I'd had enough and pledged to go back to just plain fishin'.

But the rental boats of my youth have since been condemned and I found, when rummaging through my gear, that I didn't own a bobber nor a perch hook.

Instead, my portable sporting goods warehouse was stocked with manufactured lures of every size and description. I owned stainless steel tarpon hooks, tiny gold-plated egg hooks, even a gigantic shark hook. But I no longer owned an ordinary perch hook, much less a proper rusty one.

Yes, I long to fish the weedbed with my Dad on a lazy summer afternoon as we once did. But that shall never be . . . He's gone, too, you see.

Night Creatures

We called him "Mush" and that's how I remember him—I never knew his real name.

He lived around the corner on Cranberry Avenue and was about fourteen when our family moved into the neighborhood. He was older than I by several years so naturally I looked up to him and believed just about everything he said. It was a mistake.

He was bigger than I, too, by at least a foot and perhaps forty pounds—another reason I respected him.

But the true basis for our friendship was that he was a fisherman and so was I. We hit it off from the first—as soon as he spotted the fishing rods my Dad carefully unloaded from the station wagon the day we moved in.

Still, it wasn't until we had fished Hardscrabble Creek together that I learned he was a natural born fisherman and I was not. For it was always Mush who peddled home with several large trout draped from his bicycle handlebars and me who chugged behind with only a small black sucker to show for my time.

We fished worms exclusively, of course. But his were giants compared with mine—tiny red wigglers spaded out of our vegetable garden. It bothered me that I didn't know what his kind were called; they were unlike any I'd seen. But one thing I did know was that Mush's worms always took trout. I'd seen them work. Now I was anxious to discover where he got them.

"What are those things?" I asked him one morning after he had landed his third trout and I had hooked nothing but a small shiner minnow.

"Why the guts of the dead," he grinned.

"That can't be true," I scoffed.

"It sure is," Mush insisted. "They come alive at night and crawl out around the gravestones in Highwood Cemetery."

"How do you . . . ah . . . capture them?" I wanted to know.

[37]

"That's easy," he explained. "You go to the graveyard late at night and when they ooze from the ground you grab 'em with your fingers. You've got to be quick, though, or they go back down into the corpse."

"They go back into the what?"

"The corpse . . . you know . . . the body of the dead person."

I gulped.

"Hey!" he said, "why don't we go after some tonight? I'll show you how it's done."

"I don't think so," I said weakly. "My Dad makes me go to bed at nine o'clock."

"You're saying that because you're chicken," he taunted. "If you're not you'll meet me near the old barn at midnight."

I was torn between the fear of what would happen if my Dad caught me breaking curfew, the frightening prospect of venturing into a graveyard at midnight, and the possibility of gathering enough of this obviously sure-fire trout bait to catch a good-sized trout for the first time in my life.

But after I remembered that Dad would be working late on a new machine that was being installed in the paper mill, the fisherman in me won out.

"Bring a flashlight," Mush had ordered. So before going to my room I found Dad's big five-cell—the one he used for coon hunting—and rigged a piece of clothesline as a carrying sling. If we were to wander around a graveyard at midnight I wanted the brightest light I could find.

But when I met Mush at the old barn he handed me a chunk of transparent red cellophane and a thick rubber band. "Wrap this over the lens," he directed. "White light scares 'em back into the ground before you can catch them. They don't move so fast in red light."

The cellophane idea might have been a good trick but it cut the intensity of the five-cell in half and suddenly I felt uneasy.

Then we walked deep into the cemetery, far from the glow of the street lights, to where it was black as the inside of the fruit cellar with the door closed.

The mists of a warm spring night curling from the close-mown grass and the red reflections of the flashlight beam glistening off the fog and from the tombstones was positively eerie.

Somewhere, far away in the night, a car door slammed and I shuddered, followed Mush more closely, gripping the flashlight hard.

Finally, Mush stopped near a dense hedge of thorn-bushes and aimed the light at the base of a huge granite headstone. It had a cross on top with one arm cracked away. The effect was spooky.

"See, just like I told you," Mush said evenly. And sure enough there, where the ancient stone parted the sod, slithered dozens of the same big worms that he used to catch his largest trout. Occasionally, one would be sucked back into the ground with a loud popping sound.

"The guts of the dead," Mush whispered, slipping a thumb into his mouth and flipping it off the inside of his cheek to imitate the sound.

I shuddered again and Mush showed me how to grab them and stretch them out so they couldn't snap back into their holes. Sometimes we got "doubles" when two of the things lay full-length on the surface and had become hooked together for some strange reason unknown to me.

"They're making love," Mush explained. "When they're in that condition they're easiest to catch because they don't know what's going on."

"Making love? What's that mean?"

"It's . . . well . . . ah . . . . Forget it! If you don't know you'll never understand."

Soon, in the excitement of gathering the things—"picking" Mush called it—my fright waned and I began to enjoy myself. Boy! Would I get the fish in the morning. Perhaps I'd even get lucky and hook Old Ironmouth, the trophy brown that lived in the hole under the roots of the fallen elm. Surely I'd take enough trout for supper. And I couldn't wait to see the look on the Old Man's face when he saw those monsters laying in the kitchen sink, sunset-fleshed and succulent, ready for frying in a buttered pan.

In less than an hour we had an old coffee can packed nearly full. That's when I first heard the sound, a strange, distorted, throaty sound like someone choking.

"What's that?" I whispered.

"Just the wind," Mush said, picking off another double. "Or one of those owls that live in the big swamp."

Then the noise grew louder, closer. It *was* a voice, low-pitched and quavering.

"Get . . . off . . . my . . . grave," the voice intoned, very slowly. "You're . . . walking . . . on . . . my . . . stomach!

"There," I stuttered, "you hear it now, don't you?"

Mush didn't say anything but his eyes grew wider and showed

white against the blackness of the night. I could tell he was having some heavy thoughts.

Get off my grave, the voice repeated, much closer and louder than before. *Let me sleep in peace. Get off! Or you'll join me here . . . forever.*

Mush looked at me and I at him. We couldn't move! And in that moment of indecisiveness a huge black form crashed out of the hedge. It was faceless and its arms were extended over its head. It must have been twelve feet tall!

"Geez-as!" Mush panicked. "Let's get the hell out of here."

And as we turned to run, another of the creatures lunged at us from the other direction. It was even bigger than the first!

Both creatures lurched toward us, gurgling threats and waving their arms. Mush turned to high-tail it toward the gate but his sneakers couldn't get traction on the wet grass and his feet sort of spun, like a character in a chase scene in a roadrunner cartoon.

Finally, I was crawling up Mush's back trying to get away and his feet caught the gravel of the path as we streaked through the cemetery, doing some nice broken-field running through the tombstones.

In the excitement the coffee can of bait was kicked over and the worms spilled on the ground. We left it. I left the five-cell, too, right where it dropped after the makeshift sling slipped from my shoulder when the first of the creatures came at us.

In an instant, or so it seemed at the time, we were running out the gate and down the street. Mush peeled off at Cranberry Avenue, not bothering to say good-bye, and I made tracks to the tool shed behind the garage. It was a lot tougher climbing up than sliding down but before I knew it I was on the garage roof and in through my bedroom window.

I slammed the window down and twirled the lock tight. Then I pulled the shade and drew the curtains before diving under the blankets where I shivered throughout the night.

Once, I thought I heard a car door slam and something prowling about in the garage. "Geez-as!" I thought. "They've found me."

Finally, days later it seemed, the darkness outside the window turned dull grey with morning and the coffee pot rattled on the stove downstairs.

"You're up early today," Mother said. "All dressed, too. Going fishing with Mush?"

"Maybe," I yawned, shaking out a bowl of breakfast cereal as I always did, as if nothing had happened.

Soon, Dad came down for his morning coffee and sat opposite me at the table.

"Mother," he said, talking to her but looking at me, "Mr. Price [Mr. Price was Mush's father] and I saw the strangest thing on the way home from work last night. We saw what looked like a couple of ghosts high-tailing it out of Highwood Cemetery to run right down this street."

I chomped down my cereal.

"Ghosts? That doesn't surprise me a bit," Mother said. "The girls at the Ladies Guild say the place is haunted. You should hear some of the weird tales they tell."

"What about you, son? Have you heard of anything unusual happening in that graveyard?"

"Unusual? No. I haven't heard a thing," I said, dredging the last flakes of cereal from the bowl.

"No, of course you wouldn't. You're in bed before nine o'clock every night, right?"

"Yes sir!" I stammered.

"That's precisely what I thought," he said gravely. "But just in case your mother needs you to run an errand while I'm working late at night, it might be a good idea if you had some protection, don't you think?"

I agreed it was a wise idea and Dad pushed his chair from the table to walk to the door that opened into the garage. In a few moments he returned, both arms behind his back.

"Here," he said, "this might do the trick." And he pulled the five-cell from behind his back and placed it on the table right next to the cereal box. The red cellophane was still wrapped around the lens!

I stared at it for a while, then went back to messing with the few drops of milk remaining in the bottom of my bowl, waiting for the inevitable.

"Here's your nightcrawlers, too," he said, producing the coffee can and its writhing contents and placing it on the table next to the flashlight and the cereal box.

Nightcrawlers. So that's what they were called.

"Hope you catch a big one. I'm hungry for a good meal of trout."

I knew I could, of course, for now that I had learned the name of the things and where to get them, there were two natural born fishermen in the neighborhood: Mush and *me!*

The Way to Yesterday

*H*ave you noticed, as you grow older, that time has a way of expanding and contracting, depending upon which direction it lies from today? The past seems always short, the future always long. Yesterday telescopes into the day before and that into last year and the years into decades. But tomorrow seems to take forever to come.

Star Trek freaks sometimes refer to this phenomenon as "time warp" and call the comparative differences in it the "warp factor." And for some reason I do not fully understand, hunters and fishermen appear to be more afflicted by the warp factor than are other earthlings.

Perhaps the relativity of time readily influences those of us who enjoy outdoor pursuits because our lives are guided by a time dimension that is different than that which others experience. We live from season-to-season, of course, while ordinary people live from day to day or sometimes from paycheck to paycheck.

Opening Day of trout season, for example, always seems exceedingly long in coming while the closing day in September always seems to come too soon.

And have you ever considered why those six hours between your arrival at your deer hunting camp at midnight Friday and the commencement of the legal shooting hour at dawn Saturday seems interminable, while the ten days of the full season pass in a twinkling?

Strangely, too, I seem to be cursed by the warp factor to an even greater degree than most other outdoorsmen, although I didn't realize it until recently.

An article I'd written about which particular inland lakes promised the best ice fishing for trout drew an irate response from a reader. "Brown's Lake," the reader wrote, taking me to task for the fallacious advice in the article, "contains nothing more than a few stunted panfish and an overabundance of carp." The letter went on to say that the reader knew what he was talking about because he lived year around in a shoreside cottage for more than eight years and had never seen or even heard of a trout being taken from its "scurvy" waters.

"That can't be," I thought. "Maybe he's confusing my Brown's Lake with his Brown's Lake."

But a few paragraphs later I knew that we were both referring to the same lake and it became apparent that since I'd last fished there, the warp factor had taken me over, skewing my recollections.

For although it seemed like only yesterday since I'd taken a nice catch of rainbow trout through the ice of Brown's Lake, it had actually been more like fifteen years.

Let's see, I thought, mentally calculating backwards, *my twin daughters, Lisa and Lori, were toddlers then. Now they're in college. It must be all of fifteen years, closer to twenty!*

So it was with some misgiving and embarrassment that I sat down to respond to my reader's letter.

Tempus fugit—time flies—an astute philosopher observed in ancient times. And that pithy proverb once held no meaning for me. But it does today. The Brown's Lake incident, for one, convinced me that the way to yesterday is short, the road to tomorrow long, and that time is relative to my position in it.

Time passing, too, where hunting and fishing are concerned, also appears to have the capacity to nourish memories, compelling our most pleasurable experiences to grow larger than the reality of the moment in which they happened.

I've noticed, for example, how a fair-sized white-tail buck, after it has been eaten by the hunter and the evidence thus destroyed, grows at least an extra point and adds about ten pounds for each year that's passed since it was killed.

Yes, the warp factor affects us all. It makes the snows of yesteryear deeper, the coldest winter colder, and that formidable mountain we climbed in our youth steeper, with the passing years.

Still, it is well perhaps that the warp factor works the way it does. Think of the pain that you would need to bear if you were forced *always* to remember the visceral feeling of abject disappointment that overwhelmed you when the state record brook trout spit the hook at the very moment you were to bring it to net.

And what misery you would be in, *forever*, if you had to continuously relive the intensity of the sneeze that ruined your lead precisely as the one hundredth bird was thrown from the trap house on the single day in your life that you recorded 99 straight hits.

So the warp factor, I decide, might be one of the few enigmas in life that can be reckoned with simply by doing nothing. Leave it alone! Forget it! Yesterdays are for remembering; tomorrows are for anticipating; and todays are for doing. That's the true relativity of time.

Thus thinking, I believe I'll grab my favorite fly rod after work today, drive to a delightful little trout stream near my home, and make a memory that will grow closer as the years roll by.

The Rescue

"We can't float all this gear downstream in one trip," I said. "We'll leave it and come back later."

"Someone might steal it," said Karl.

"Nobody's going to come across this stuff way back here in the bush," I said. "You're overly cautious because you work at the reformatory, guarding all those incorrigible delinquents."

"The youths I work with are now called 'residents,'" he admonished. "But I swear one of those guys that passed here in the yellow canoe was one of my ex-cons, out on parole for burglary."

"Ex-*con?*"

"Excuse me . . . one of my . . . ah . . . former clients—an ex-*resident*. And if he's who I think he is, this gear isn't safe. He once picked the lock on my office door, then picked the lock on my desk drawer, and relocked them afterwards, just so he could get to a carton of cigarettes I kept there. And he doesn't even smoke!"

"Do you think he recognized you?"

"Probably . . . He's observant, as all cons . . . ah . . . ex-residents are."

"Why do you keep correcting yourself?" I wanted to know.

"It's those damn social workers," Karl explained. "They think all human beings are sweethearts. So we're required to label those no-good . . . ah . . . those wayward youths in more respectable terms."

"What's wrong with that?"

"By the time they get to me," Karl said, "they're three-time losers. The court system nowadays will only incarcerate those who've fouled up again and again."

"All right. You've convinced me. Somebody . . . identity unknown . . . might steal the gear. What do we do?"

"Well . . ." Karl said, "I'm off work tomorrow. I could guard the camp overnight. You take the others downstream in the boat, drive

[45]

home, get the motor repaired, and come back for the gear and me tomorrow."

"Sounds good," I said. "But are you sure you can manage? It's going to drop below freezing tonight. It might even snow. And what if your ex-inmate . . . ah . . . ex-client comes back and sees one of his former guards unarmed?"

"Don't worry," Karl said. "I can handle that dude. Like most criminals, he won't confront anyone with an overpowering personality."

"God!"

"One thing . . ." Karl said.

"Yes?"

"Are there any snakes around? Or bear? I've never spent a night alone this far back in the bush."

"If there are," I said blithely, "they're too smart to be roaming around in weather like this."

And I was right. For a churning front had moved in as we'd talked. It brought snow, sleet and driving rain—an unseasonable gift from northeastern Canada. And it was not unexpected!

In early May, for the opening weekend of trout fishing at Camp One Rapids Pool, weather conditions are always unpredictable. Some years we find balmy temperatures and clean, sunbathed skies—shirtsleeve fishing weather. Other years might bring what we refer to as "unsettled" conditions, anything from late storms out of the Arctic to drenching torrential rain—unappealing even for Eskimos or Patagonians, whatever the case might be.

This year, conditions on the Popple River were far from ideal. And our annual excursion had gotten off to an uncertain start; an intensely cold winter featuring less than normal snowfall had restricted streamflow to near-drought levels. The activity of the rapids, ordinarily singing and bubbling, had been reduced to a muted sluicing of the slow and shallow water among the midstream rock.

Downstream, gravel bars normally hidden under several feet of spring runoff, this year were exposed. And deadheads—sunken remnants of the great logging drives of fifty years ago—now lay just under the surface; if you wandered from the channel, boating became hazardous, to say the least.

It had taken three upstream trips to transport our party of ten and its gear from the landing to our Camp One Rapids campsite. The submerged deadheads, unseen until contact with them revealed their presence, had caused broken shear pins on the first two trips. Then, on the third, at a long sweeping bend a hundred yards downstream of the rapids, the motor prop had shattered on an underwater boulder.

Without the motor, it would be an impossible task to get the several hundred pounds of gear back downstream in a reasonable time, for the Popple is a high-gradient stream and it would be difficult to row against the formidable current on the upstream trips.

"Are you sure you can manage overnight, Karl?" I asked.

"There's plenty of food, and plenty of this," he said, holding aloft a full quart of our favorite chill-fighter.

As I piled the others into the boat for the trip downstream, Karl huddled over the smoldering campfire and fed small twigs into the sodden coals. The twigs would flare for an instant and momentarily die! Wet snow had soaked most of the downed wood; the wind was rising, turning the wetness into an encumbering glaze, and hailstones pelted against Karl's rain poncho—he was in for a miserable night.

We waved good-bye and Karl, smiling forlornly, toasted our departure with a blue-enameled cup filled with chill-fighter.

"Are you sure you want to stay here?" I asked before casting off. "Not even Dillinger would be pillaging on a night like this."

"No," said Karl. "I'll stay. This is something I have to do."

"O.K.," I said, with a flash of sadistic inspiration, "but watch out for the bear. I lied to you. They enjoy coming out in weather like this."

Karl grimaced, then turned to feed more twigs into the fire.

Early the next morning I made the rounds of all the marinas, looking for a replacement prop for the ancient outboard motor. None had any. But at the last place on my list the salesman said, "This piece of machinery must be thirty years old. If you want a new prop I can order it from a supply house in Minneapolis . . . It shouldn't take more than three weeks."

"Three weeks?"

"Yeah. I got connections."

"Have you a rental?" I inquired, explaining my problem of boating upstream in low flow.

"I'll rent this motor for $15 a day," he said. "It has a short shaft and the prop won't drag bottom."

Overnight, the access road to the river landing had decomposed into a morass of slippery red clay, typical of the area's soils. We'd have a hard time traveling back to the highway without bogging down and I hoped no other vehicle came in to rut the road into even poorer condition before we returned from the river.

I secured the rental motor to the transom, pushed off from the bank, started the motor with a single pull and headed upstream. Ten yards out I heard the familiar dull *thunk!* and the motor raced wildly. "Damn!" Barely underway and I'd broken another shear pin. More exasperating was the realization that I'd forgotten to bring extras.

I beached the craft and sat fuming over my forgetfulness. If I drove to the nearest town, which was about twenty miles away, it was an even bet that I'd get stuck either on the way out or on the return trip. Karl was waiting and I knew he wouldn't attempt to walk out. He didn't know the country and the overnight storm had soaked the swamplands on either side of the stream. Hiking would be impossible.

Finally, I rummaged through the car seeking a wire, a nail, a coathanger—anything—with which to fashion a makeshift shear pin. Nothing! I sat dejectedly on the river bank and contemplated my next move.

The sky was clear by now and the temperature was creeping into the high thirties. A red-tailed hawk drifted in the updrafts, hunting, and a slight southeast wind rustled the curled parchment of the leaves which clung to the ranks of scrub oak marshaling up the ridgeline. Scrub oak? Of course! I had a pocket knife; I'd *carve* a shear pin.

Several minutes of patient whittling produced a useable shear pin. It held until the halfway point when the whirling prop ticked the gravel bottom, shattering the wooden pin. Hastily I carved another.

The river was rising, now, fed by the rain and melting snow of yesterday's storm. The flat-bottomed river boat floated easily over the deadheads, submerged rocks and the gravel bars.

Karl was pacing on the bank, the gear stowed and neatly piled around him.

"Sandberg to the rescue," I called as I cut the throttle. "How's the castaway?"

"It's about time you got here," he grumbled.

"How was the sleeping?" I said cheerfully, not wishing to explain that I'd been negligent enough to arrive without replacement shear pins.

"You'd be surprised what goes on up here at night. I heard all kinds of crazy sounds. Once I looked out of the tent and saw what appeared to be a bear. It went away. Another time I thought I heard that ex-con rummaging around. He left, too."

"No wonder you heard strange sounds," I said, pointing to the empty quart of chill-fighter that was laying beside the gear. "You polished off that jug all by yourself?"

"I sure as hell didn't feed it to the bear," said Karl.

We loaded the gear, Karl climbed atop the pile, and an hour later we cruised into the landing. And, on the trip out, the extra weight of the gear allowed the car to surge through the muddy ruts of the road with relative ease.

The next morning, when I returned the rental motor, I explained my ingenuity with the carved oak shear pins.

The salesman shook his head and laughed. "Why didn't you use these?" He reached over the metal cowling and pulled a magnetic box off the motor. It was about the size of an aspirin container and painted bright red.

"What's that?"

He smirked as he opened the tiny box, exposing its contents—a half dozen shiny, unblemished metal shear pins.

The Sash-Weight Bait Affair

Most outdoorsmen are aware of Ed Zern. He's the reason a major outdoor magazine is usually read back end to. For Zern reports his delightful carryings-on in "Exit Laughing," a column that has usurped the very last page of the magazine for many years.

One item in a Zern column caused my angler's blood to race faster than if I'd received an intravascular feeding of Canadian brook trout water.

"Like most fishermen," Zern wrote, "I'm awfully tired of reading about that 39½ pound brown trout caught in *Loch Awe* in Scotland in 1866 and wish somebody would catch a bigger one, which isn't likely to happen, of course, as it was probably an Atlantic salmon and/or stuffed with sash weights."

The key phrase was "stuffed with sash weights." I didn't know what they were but if giant brown trout ate them they would make a good addition to my tackle box.

After some preliminary searching, which was unfruitful, I wrote Zern:

Dear Mr. Zern:
   One item in your recent "Exit Laughing" column really intrigued me. I'm talking, of course, about the sash-weight bait you allege the World's record brown trout was stuffed with when caught way back in 1866— I've been looking for a sure-fire bait like that for a long, long time.
   Unfortunately, I haven't been able to find any of them in our local tackle stores. I even tried all two of the bait shops in Algoma, Wisconsin, to no avail.
   In fact, the elderly proprietor in the largest of the two establishments—a 12 ft. by 18 ft. garage with an overhead door that was off its track—said he'd fished as far south as Two Creeks and as far north as Gill's Rock without ever having seen a sash-weight bait, much less one that had actually caught a brown trout.

"But," I protested, "Ed Zern, the famous outdoor writer said . . ."
At the mention of your name the old guy interrupted with a fit of
uncontrollable laughter. "Sonny," he gurgled, that fella Zern knows
how to write good, but he don't know about fishin'. Maybe he ain't as
well traveled as I am. I've fished Dunbar, Athelstane and Bear Creek as
well as Gill's Rock and Two Creeks, and I've never seen a sash-weight
bait anywhere. Not even one!
Mr. Zern, I'd sure appreciate it if you would set this matter straight.
Is there really a sash-weight bait? And if so where can I buy one? I'd
like to take at least one good trout in my life.

Sincerely,
Walt Sandberg

I posted the letter and sat back to oil my fishing gear in anticipation of Zern's reply. Three weeks later I received it:

Dear Walt:
Thanks for your thoughtful letter. I am having a gross of Little Giant
sash-weight baits airmailed to you as soon as possible. Expect them
soon, C.O.D.

Sincerely,
Ed Zern

I got out the oil can and worked on my light spinning gear with renewed frenzy.

A few days later, the package arrived—airmail C.O.D. Although I've no way of knowing for sure, it must have come from Zern, for it was postmarked Scarsdale, New York, his home town.

I could tell right off that the word *gross* in his letter did not *mean* quantity, as I had originally supposed, it meant *condition!* For the package contained only a single lure which was truly an aberration—I'd never seen anything like it before.

And I could tell, too, from the dent it put in my steel-toe safety shoe when I accidentally dropped it, that it was designed as a deep diver.

The thing was about a foot long, painted bright yellow with dime-sized green and blue spots, and snelled to a three-eighths-inch hawser. A pair of pheasant wings, dyed chartreuse, I presumed to be the hackle. And the over-sized hook braised to its keel might have been commissioned by the same moviemakers who had filmed *Jaws*.

It was obvious I couldn't handle Zern's device with light spinning tackle. So I rummaged in the attic for an old five-and-a-half-foot solid glass, one-piece, musky rod. Attached to it was an ancient level-wind bait-casting reel tangled with 50-pound test braided dacron line.

Excitedly, I bent the snelled hawser to the line in an unwieldy clinch knot and headed for my favorite trout stream. There, I clambered up the highest bank I could find and flung the lure bodily over the river.

That's when I realized, too late, that I'd violated Angling Rule Number 1: Always examine your line prior to use! For once the lure was airborne there was no turning back. An unremembered knot caught against a nick in the reel post and whipped the line into a monstrous bird's nest, the writhing coils of which lashed my hand and wrist tightly to the rod butt. This caused the lure to twang to a dead stop far out over the water.

That's when I discovered, also too late, that I'd violated Angling Rule Number 2: Always pre-test your drag! Unused for several seasons, it had rusted tight.

The momentum of the skyrocketing lure, combined with the unyielding frozen drag, jerked the entire assembly, with me inexorably knotted to it, into a trajectory that put us far out over the river, like a living ground-to-ground missile, directly amidships of a passing canoe.

The bowman, a portly old gentleman with a sun-reddened bald spot that was easily distinguished from my vantage point overhead, must have been a World War II Navy veteran. For when he chanced to look up he shouted: "The kamikazes are coming! The kamikazes are coming!" and promptly abandoned ship.

That's when *he* violated Angling Rule Number 3: Always remain with your craft! For the minor tidal wave that accompanied our splashdown near the canoe almost drowned the poor guy.

Unfortunately, the sternman remained aboard. He fished me out of the water, introduced himself as an inspector with the Department of Environmental Protection, and fined me, on the spot, $25 and costs. It seems that under an obscure provision of the 1894 Rivers and Harbors Act when my gear, with me attached to it, hit the water we became an injurious, foreign substance in a public waterway.

But he did cut me loose.

Later, I considered hiring a tow truck to winch the bait from the mucky bottom, but managed instead to grapple it out with a pair of logging tongs thoughtfully loaned by an old lumberjack who lived nearby. Then I packaged it up and dispatched it back across the continent to Scarsdale, C.O.D. of course.

And Zern refused it!

Anyone out there looking for a sure-fire killer bait on trout? It's reposing now, in my backyard. And the EPA guy says if I don't get rid of it soon, he'll cite me again. This time for operating a sanitary landfill without a permit.

Snowflake Speckles

*I*t snowed hard through the night. Hard and wet. The rapids breathed frozen mist just before daylight and I reached out of my sleeping bag long enough to stir a pine knot into the embers. Soon the fire was warming our black-bottomed coffee pot. Trout were rising in the tail of the pool.

Sourdough makings had been working all night in a crock buried near my feet. I pulled it out, cracked two eggs, and folded them into the batter.

Breakfast was sizzling bacon slabs and sourdough pancakes floating in warm maple syrup with a dollop of brandy for flavor.

After the coffee was finished I reached under the plastic lean-to and unrolled my waders. Away from the fire it was colder and my fingers blotched red and white, then blue as I tied on a Hornberg. I rummaged in my duffle and found a pair of old jersey gloves. I put on the left glove. It felt better.

Gordy took another long, warming pull from the coffee pot while I jumped to the big rock and false-cast over the pool. *Swish! Zing!* The torpedo taper whipped through the guides and sliced through the mists.

"It looks like a good opening day," Gordy said as he jumped up beside me, flicking his two-pound test monofilament line into the eddy and slowly working a *Mepps* spinner.

"Snowing like this?" I hooted.

"Yes," said Gordy, "Popple River brookies even rise to snowflakes early in the season."

"Snowflakes?" I laughed. "Is that anything like snipe hunting? Or sending a guy in search of a left-handed monkey wrench?"

Gordy sucked the ice from his rod tip and grimaced as his tongue stuck to the steel guide. "Brookies are hungry this time of year," he explained, "and when snow hits the water they think it's a hatch."

"You're nuts!" I scoffed.

He flicked the spinner out, into the rings of a rise. The line stopped and he set the hook.

"See what I mean?" he said. "They rise to snowflakes but won't take dry flies this early in the season. I've tried white midges to test them. Streamers and spinners work best, fished just under the surface."

I twitched the Hornberg. Soon we had a pair of fit, ten-inch native brook trout flopping on the bank.

Ray "Gordy" Gordon knows Wisconsin's Popple River like no one else. His father—Old Ray, we call him—fished in it soon after the virgin white pine forest had been cut over by early loggers. Old Ray tells of "catching-up" a fry of forty to fifty speckled beauties in the hour between church services and Sunday dinner in the 1920's. He worked in the woods along the river for over fifty years, starting as an ice boy who watered the tracks for the horse-drawn logging sleds.

Old Ray gave his son a love of the Northwoods and the river and a curiosity about wild things. Now the son has the seasoning of three generations and more knowledge of the river than the father.

Gordy first brought me to Camp One Rapids to fish snowflake speckles on a blustery Opening Day about twenty years ago. Ever since, the first weekend in May finds us back. It is always the same: cold mists, snow, and rising trout.

To get there we travel Highway 101 off Highway 8 from the village of Armstrong Creek in Forest County. Then through the tiny crossroads village of Fence into the back country on an old railroad grade, rutted and unused for many years. A weed-tangled field marks Camp One, a logging site abandoned by the Goodman Lumber Company—Old Ray's employer—in the late 1920's.

We park near the overgrown outline of a bunkhouse, pull the canoe around the bunker-like remnants of a root cellar, and grunt our gear down a steep hogback to a long, slow-moving bend of the river.

Camp One Rapids is a mile upstream. And that mile is itself an adventure. The Popple has been designated a "wild" river by the state legislature. It is a free-flowing river with clean, high quality waters and most of its length is in near wilderness condition.

If the time is right we know we'll see a beaver on the trip upstream and often a porcupine or a white-tail deer. Sometimes we see a nesting pair of mallard or redhead ducks. Once we saw a black bear enjoying a chilly bath and an otter sliding down a slippery log.

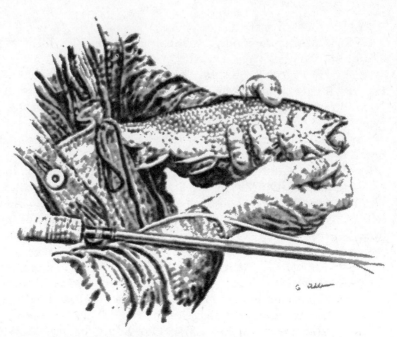

Gordy cleaned our twin speckles as soon as we landed them. "Look," he said, sorting their stomach contents with the point of a rusty pocket knife. "Minnows and nymphs. No bugs."

By now the sun had burned off the morning mist. Light snow was still falling. And above the trees we saw a "snowbow," which is similar to a rainbow. But with May sunlight and ice crystals in the air the phenomenon is more alive than the July thundershower kind; more iridescent; and more worthy of remembering.

Gordy washed the trout and put them in a nest of early sweet fern, fringed with arbutus. "That's lunch," he said. "Now let's go after a trophy."

"I don't know," I yawned. "That noisy bittern kept me awake half the night. Then the frogs."

"Yeah," Gordy smiled. "But wasn't it great?"

I downed my coffee and watched the tannin-dyed Popple River bubbling through the rapids. That, I knew, was reply enough.

The path to the upper pool winds among huge, windblown white cedars and enormous stream-tumbled boulders. The boulders, carried here from Canada by the glaciers more than twelve thousand years ago, look velvety and soft from a covering of centuries of liverwort and moss. We teetered over a natural bridge of these gigantic stepping stones to cross a feeder creek, and followed the river upstream into some towering yellow birch. It was quiet but we could still hear a muted sluicing of water over the rapids a quarter mile back.

Then I saw it. An eagle. He was gliding upstream on a hunt over a slow stretch of river. "Look!" I cried.

"Ten years ago there were many more," Gordy said.

Above Camp One Rapids the river comes through flatland swamps and sweeps slowly along huge, granitic rocks strewn haphazardly in the stream. Occasionally the rocks on either bank are so numerous the flow is constricted to a fast-running trough. A deep hole usually forms near the tail and the turbulent waters pour in hordes of trout food to the slower bottom water. Here, big trout establish holding lies.

We stopped at the head of the first run. I was about to dunk my trusty Hornberg. Gordy shook his head and snapped a Number 3 *Mepps* to his ultralight spinning line. "Want big fish, fish big lures," he said.

I fingered through my fly box and came out with a big, showy Spuddler. Ray nodded and led the way into the river where a rock cut the current into separate runs.

"You take that side," he pointed.

"Shallow or deep?" I motioned. "Seems to me they'll be hugging bottom here."

"Still snowing," Gordy replied.

We cast out together and worked both sides of the rock. I held my rod tip high to keep the fly just under the surface. The Spuddler twitched downstream in the current and I hand-lined it back to keep it alive. Each cast cut through snowflakes and I could only lay the fly by random guesswork because the water was too fast to hold the rings of a rise.

I cast up and across and twirled the fly around the rock. Then mid-run and let it come tumbling straight down. Then bankside, slicing it under the budding alders. And again; altering the casting pattern after each series.

After two dozen casts I said acidly, "Your snowflake speckles have hibernated."

"Easy," Gordy said as he worked his spinner slowly around his half of the run. "There's a lot of morning left."

Suddenly, as the Spuddler swung into the downstream pocket

formed by the rock, a huge swirl engulfed the fly. "Tailing," Gordy said softly. "Cast again; same spot."

The brookie hit on the next pass, slapping its tail out of the water and nosing down to gulp the fly hungrily just inches under the surface. I felt the fish hook itself and stripped line and let it run.

The fish pulled downstream, causing the hanging line to loop, unnoticed, around my leg when it turned. I tugged but the line wouldn't give. "Snagged!" I fumed.

"Yeah," Gordy laughed. "You've snagged yourself."

I disentangled the line and felt the fish bore cross-stream. "Got him!" I said.

Two more rushes and it tired. I floated it in on its side and crooked my thumb and forefinger through the gills, sweeping it from the water.

It was a dazzling male brook trout. His belly shined bone white. Fluorescent orange ventral fins set off the jeweled red and blue spots on his flanks. Topside he was a shimmering charcoal green.

"Nice fish," Gordy said. "Sixteen inches at least."

"Pretty good size," I agreed, "for having to live on a low-calorie diet of snowflakes."

The Last Raid

The float plane was bouncing in the updrafts just over the treetops, plodding along at near-stall, when a sudden glint of water beneath its nose told me that I had found what I was seeking—a secluded Northwoods beaver pond allegedly loaded with native brook trout. The pilot banked into a side-roll to study the landing area for obstructions, then hit the throttles and pulled the stick, sending the plane into a stomach-compressing power climb.

"Just like in der vore," he chortled in a thick, Germanic accent, his eyes glinting wildly behind the goggles.

I swallowed the metallic-tasting fluid that had been building in my throat and said nothing.

"Don't vorry," he assured me, "I can land der aorcraft . . ."

"Yes, I know," I interrupted, smiling wanly. "You can land the aircraft in a soup bowl of borscht."

"Nein," he shook his head and whipped the plane into a looping bank that corkscrewed it out of the climb at an altitude of about four thousand feet. "Not a bowl, a zoop-*plate*. Und dis pond is not a zoop-plate. Dis pond is vorst."

With that, he brought the nose down and aimed the plane at the treetops for the next pass. Several of my internal organs again collapsed and a demanding voice within me nagged: *How in the hell did I get into this?*

A week earlier, during the August trout fishing doldrums, I had overheard pieces of a conversation while waiting for my car to be serviced at a crossroads garage in a tiny Northwoods village nearby. Although the yammering of an air-operated impact wrench made hearing difficult, the few phrases I managed to discern sent the pressure of my angler's blood soaring: . . . *huge beaver pond . . . pulled out a four-pound speckle . . . no access . . . hasn't been fished in years.*

"Who are those guys?" I inquired of the mechanic after the two well-dressed men drove away in a sparkling white luxury automobile.

"Big wheels from Chicago. I think they're members of the Hartley Lake Club."

I knew about the Hartley Lake Club, of course; everyone who fished the area knew of it. The members-only club owned twenty-four hundred acres of pristine northern woodlands which encompassed several lakes and portions of two Class I trout streams. I'd cast envious eyes across its locked gates dozens of times. But I never entered because the club had the reputation of swiftly prosecuting trespassers and asking the county judge to envoke maximum penalties. Since the judge fished the club waters several times each season as a guest, he was generally happy to oblige.

Still, the vision of tangling with a trophy brook trout of four pounds or more kept pulsing through my mind. Upon arriving home, I found the proper topographic map and studied it to determine the location of a "huge beaver pond" with "no access" that even club members hadn't "fished in years."

In minutes I had pinpointed the only possible pond site: a lowland basin of several hundred acres ringed by steep glacial ridges through which meandered the largest of the trout streams. The map, which hadn't been updated in many years, showed a small blue patch above the confluence of a feeder creek and the larger stream. Perhaps the beaver had enlarged the dam, impounding more water, and had created a new lake where native brook trout, living unmolested, had grown to trophy proportions.

Confident that I had identified the pond that the members of the Hartley Lake Club had been reveling about, I sought to find a route over which I might hike in without being detected.

The prospects looked bleak. A trail terminated on a ridge about a mile from the pond, otherwise the area was roadless. And judging by the map, it would be impossible to wade in through the surrounding bog. Anyway, it would be better if I journeyed to the pond by floating downstream in a canoe! In this state, navigable waterways are in public trust—they belong to all; and anglers who stay midstream can fish without fear of being cited for trespass. Only if they encroach on bordering private lands are they subject to arrest and prosecution.

Unfortunately, I noted that several portages would be required if I were to float to the pond by canoe. Since occupied guest cottages were located both upstream and downstream of the pond, there was a good chance that I'd be apprehended by the club's security patrol long before I reached my destination. I decided there was only one legal way to get to the Hartley Lake Club's brook trout: I'd drop into the pond from the air.

That same afternoon I walked into the cluttered office of the Northern Lights Floatplane Service and said to the manager, "I need a daring pilot, but a good one."

"All our pilots are good," he said, repeating the bush pilot's favorite banality; "bad ones don't last long in this business."

After I explained my mission, he thought a moment and said, "I've got just the man for you, Ludwig von Haffen. Everyone calls him Colonel Klink, like the guy on TV."

"Why do they call him that?"

"You'll see."

Early on the morning of the flight I carried my gear to the floatplane dock and approached the wiry, furtive man who was packing there. He wore a cracked and faded leather jacket and a military-style aviator's cap, the crown of which flopped over his ears like bat wings. Goggles, the type with the round eyepieces, hung on a strap around his neck and he chewed a stubby cigar. Altogether he was the archetypal image of daredevil bush pilots everywhere.

"Mr. von Haffen?"

"Ja, Mein Herr," he clicked his heels and leaned toward me in a half-bow.

I showed him the topographic map and explained about the beaver pond. "Don't vorry," he said. "I vas a Messerschmitt pilot in der Vorld Vore. I made many secret raids."

"What brought you to the Northwoods?"

"In Germany, after der vore, dey vouldn't let me fly der big airliners."

"Vye . . . ah . . . why not?"

"Dey say I crock up too many aorcrafts," said Colonel Klink, chuckling at his joke and clapping me on the back.

Once airborne, Colonel Klink placed the topographic map in his lap and dead-reckoned a course toward the pond. When I expressed concern that the pond might be full of beaver cuttings, snags and downed trees which would prevent landing, he replied with bravado, "Don't vorry, I can land der aorcraft in a zoop-plate of borscht."

My doubts about Colonel Klink's flying ability evaporated on the second pass over the pond. He swept the plane in low over the treetops, cut the airspeed, and simply plopped down into the water. In minutes I had assembled my gear and was standing on a float, ready to fish. The Colonel braced his back against a strut on the other float, stretched out, adjusted his cigar, and appeared to be settling in for a nap.

I cast a *Mepps* spinner into the water where I guessed the flooded stream channel to be, and two turns of the reel handle brought a resounding strike.

"It's a good one!" I yelled. The Colonel merely shrugged into a more comfortable position and ignored me.

The fish circled toward midpond and then streaked for the beaver dam. Abruptly, the line snubbed tight against the reel spool and turning the handle brought no other action than the clicking of the drag. Snagged!

"I'm going to wade to the dam and try to work him loose from the other side," I told the Colonel, who nodded and yawned.

Holding the rod high overhead and reeling to hold the line taut, I teetered along the top of the dam and tugged tentatively. A slight whipping movement indicated that the fish was still hooked and had probably wound the end of the line around an underwater beaver cutting.

As I worked the rod-tip to free the fish I glanced up to see the Colonel standing on the float, gesturing wildly and repeatedly pointing at me. Occasionally, he would cup his hands around his mouth to shout something, but I couldn't hear him over the sound of rushing water through the looseness of the dam.

"Ah, ha!" I thought. "He's finally recognized what a fine fish I have on and he's giving me encouragement."

I waved at him, laughed, and yelled: "Yes. It's a beauty, Colonel. A real beauty."

That's when I heard the brush crack behind me and a low, gravelly voice say exuberantly, "Gotcha, buddy!"

I looked over my shoulder, still working the rod to free my trophy brook trout, to see two men dressed in camouflage clothing burst out of the alders. The embroidered patches on the shoulders of their jackets read: *Hartley Lake Club—Security Patrol.*

"Hi fellas," I said brightly. "You guys sure raise some good-sized fish. Wait until I bring this one in; then we'll talk. O. K.?"

"You won't bring any fish in, buddy," said the larger of the pair.

"You're under arrest. You're trespassing."

"Wait a minute," I said. "This is a navigable stream. I came in by air, as you can see. I haven't put a foot on your land."

"You've got two feet on it, now." He gestured downward.

"Can't we work this out?" I inquired weakly.

"We figured this would happen," he explained. "We figured once you local-yokels heard about the brook trout you'd come in by air. We were on our way as soon as we heard your plane buzzing overhead."

By now, the Colonel, using an old canoe paddle he carried in the cockpit, had maneuvered the plane into the deepest part of the pond about fifteen yards from our position on the dam. I waved him off. If he beached, the security patrol might apprehend him, too. They might even impound the plane.

Instead, the Colonel called to me from his sanctuary, barely able to contain his elation, rubbing his palms together in glee. "Der ambush. Just like in der vore. Vot you tink?"

"I think," I said, "that this is my last raid."

The Colonel responded with a wave and a maniacal laugh. Then he adjusted his goggles, strapped himself into his seat, and roared off to buzz the pond in a wild farewell."

"Nazis!" the big guard spat into the placid waters of the pond and yanked roughly on my arm. "I thought we got rid of you guys in 1945."

Irritably, I pulled away, noticing for the first time the old fishing shirt I had chosen to wear that day: dark brown, of worsted cotton, tailored with epaulets in a military cut.

Stalking Those Long-Lost Neurons

*E*ver since I read somewhere that those of us approaching thirty or creeping somewhat over it lose more than a hundred thousand neurons each and every day, I've been up-tight.

Then, when I read in another article that those of us who are outdoorsmen and spend a lot of time in the sun lose, during each hour of such overexposure, several thousand more, I got up-tighter still.

But when I read, in yet another article, that those who drink martinis—a heavenly elixir of imported English gin, over ice, nothing more—will lose double their ordinary daily quota of the things for each stemmed glassful of the juniper-tasting brew so happily ingested, I began to really worry.

First of all, I didn't even know what a neuron was. . . . But here I sat, losing them . . . by scads . . . daily.

And I knew, too, from past experience, that whatever they were, I, of all people, couldn't afford to lose any, not even one.

I pondered how this situation could upset my later life. If I waited to retire until age sixty-five, I would, at the triplicate rate I was losing the things, inadvertently slosh-off about 3.29 Quads of whatever they were (a Quad being the equivalent of a quadrillion of anything and the latest buzzword among energy-informed ecologists and engineers).

That seemed too much.

Therefore, I subtracted 0.27×10^9 of them to allow for leap years (that last symbolism being what's called a "scientific notation," representing something I have yet to figure out).

And that, of course, was still too much.

Right there, I decided to retire instead at fifty-two, at which time I would have lost several billion less of the things, thus conserving them which, in this age of impending shortages, is the patriotic thing to do.

That problem disposed of, I concluded it time to find out what it was that I was losing at such an alarming rate. I had only to turn to the "N" section of my dictionary. It stated: "neu-ron (noo'ron) n. *Physiol.* The fundamental cellular unit of the nervous system; also called a *nerve cell.*"

Oh, no! I could see I was in for real trouble. Imagine! My brain, without my prior knowledge or consent, merely because heredity had niched me as a lower middle-aged outdoorsman who occasionally sipped the nectar of the Celtic gods in bright sunlight, electing to indiscriminately toss around my nerve cells like some mad Russian diner eating spaghetti with chopsticks—*my* nerve cells.

I could plainly see that if I retired at fifty-two, my brain would ultimately diminish itself to the size of a nut, probably pistachio, somewhat smaller than the peanut which, for reasons known only to turncoat Yankee liberals, appears to be the vogue-nut of the day.

And if that indeed happened, I clearly saw, too, that I could never again expect to summon the nerve to pot a squirrel from a treetop with my 12-gauge full-choke using Number 6's. Nor could I ever again expect to brazenly entice a native brook trout into slurping up my nightcrawler on a recently impounded beaver pond.

Immediately, I decided against retiring at fifty-two and upped the date to forty-five, at which time I would be minus only an additional Quad or two of my suddenly precious neurons.

Then, on a lazy Tuesday evening in midsummer, as I mourned my lost neurons before re-runs on the tube, I accidentally stayed tuned long enough to watch the late-evening news. There, in all her lisping glory, was that self-styled expert on twenty-first-century affairs. Barbara Walters, cryptically spewing some soul-shattering tidings:

"Scientists now believe neurons contain quantities of a substance called RNA which controls memory."

"O.K., Barbie-baby," I pleaded. "Give it to me . . . I can take it."

"RNA," she obliged, "has been injected into white rats in the laboratory. The injected rats were found to be faster learners than their non-injected control group. They seemed to remember better, too."

"Rats!" I echoed, for I had always been a slow learner and an even poorer rememberer, particularly when it comes to completing household chores before going trout fishing, grouse hunting, crab trapping, smelt seining, frog whopping, skeet shooting, dog training, goldenrod grub picking, cross-country skiing, crow shooting, or any of the other myriad peripheral duties of the sometime outdoorsman.

If what Ms. Walters had reported was indeed scientific fact, it followed that I had been born with fewer neurons than other people. And seeing that everyone loses the things at the same rate, didn't it mean that I would run out of mine before anyone else?

Of course it did!

And if that was true, as is surely was, it meant that I would someday forget how to get back to all those secret hunting and fishing spots I tricked others into showing me how to get to over the years. (They took me to them, I suppose, because they figured my less-than-total recall would preclude my remembering how to spy my way back.)

That settled it. I just had to find some neurons to add to and replace my ever-diminishing supply. But where does one get a new allotment of neurons?

A department store perhaps? I tried several. None had any. But one courteous salesperson suggested that I might wish to order them from their nearest catalog warehouse in Minneapolis, for which an additional charge would be assessed for handling, postage and sales tax.

"Salesperson," I said, "I haven't lost that many neurons yet."

Next, my quest took me to the purveyors of the exotic in the Plaza Shopping Mall downtown. This is the core of the inner city where the developer demolished twelve square blocks of lovely red-brick buildings which were rented by small businessmen, used one block to put up a high-rise, high-rental retail complex, and left the remaining eleven blocks fallow—one-half in Hiroshima-like rubble and one-half in sterile, unproductive, asphalt-covered parking lot.

But all I found in the Plaza were fastfood stands, fabric shops, record stores, a fly-by-night "genuine" native-American jewelry outlet, and the local franchise for Hedrick's of Hollywood lingerie.

Fortunately, Hedrick's was celebrating its grand opening and live models pranced about in scanties among a tasteful display of our nation's latest nuclear attack missiles, which the local recruiter had been induced into setting up in the commons as a drawing card.

After several hours of peering at the Hedrick models undulating diaphanously through the nose cones, I determined that neither they nor those who had developed our nuclear arsenal had many neurons to spare either.

Still, the stop wasn't entirely wasted, for I took a moment to browse through the new shipment of specialty magazines at the newsstand. There, among dozens of publications devoted to running, I spotted several interesting titles: *The Grass Carp Angler* was loaded with where-to information about this prolific and exciting gamefish; *The 'In Reptilian* contained an important feature article about hunting garter snakes close to home; and *The Urban Climber* had a round-up piece, which included route maps, about the world's highest unclimbed skyscrapers.

When I arrived home, I flopped down in my zebra-hide sling chair, kicked off my imported alligator-leather boots, turned the air conditioner to "high cooling" and lolled out to further ponder my problem. And only then did I notice that I'd disturbed the stack of unread mail which I'd disconcertingly tossed on the smooth, certified-agate top of my elephant-legged coffee table during these past weeks when I'd been worrying over my lost neurons.

Then, as fate would have it, a Christmas catalog from a mail order sporting goods store slickly and colorfully slid its way to the top of the pile . . . What caught my eye I suppose, was the cover painting—an animal sporting the white tail of *Odocoileus virginianus borealis* and the antlers of *Odocoileus hemionus hemionus* . . . a truly representative portrait of popular zoology in action.

Despite the cover, I picked up the publication and flipped through its enticing pages: where more likely a place to find the exciting, the expensive, the unusual, the absurd . . . the *neuron.*

Excitedly, I saw that the catalog offered everything. Here was a pair of elephant hair bracelets ($89.95). There was a brass-tipped, hand-waxed, solid ashwood hiking staff ($29.95). And here was, too, an ivory, scrimshawed backgammon game in an elk-hide case ($639.95). There was even an 1,800-pound cast-bronze statue of a rhinoceros complete with enameled tick birds pecking at its back ($3296.95 F.O.B. Dallas, TX 75221).

But there were no neurons.

What was I to do?

Then it hit me. Of course! Why hadn't I thought of it before. The want-ads.

Hurriedly I dialed the phone and asked for Ms. Friendly Ad-Taker:

[67]

"Whadayawand?" Ms. Friendly Ad-Taker responded after the fifth ring.

"I'd like to place an ad in Category 38," I replied.

"Waz that?"

"Category 38 is 'Wanted.' "

"It is? Then why call me . . . call the cops," Ms. Friendly Ad-Taker giggled.

"I wish to place an ad in Category 38 . . . Wanted," I repeated calmly.

"You don't have to shout, mister, I ain't one of them drunken handicaps working in that noisy city room."

"The ad will say," I declared in my cultured ex-Marine drill sergeant monotone: "*Wanted.* Surplus neurons in any condition. Will pay top dollar. Call Walt. 433-1630. Anytime. Day or night."

"Got it," she said. "But what's a neuron?"

"If you have to ask," I said, chagrined, "you obviously don't have any."

"Kiss-off, mister," she replied. "I'll have you know that I'm a perfect 36–22–36 and I've got all of what you're looking for. But I don't believe my supervisor will accept your obscene ad in Category 38."

"What?"

"This newspaper has a reputation to protect, mister. We only accept obscene ads in Category 19."

"This is not an obscene ad," I explained. "It's . . . it's . . . a supplication."

"We don't have any category for that either, mister. If you want your pornography to run it goes in Category 19. Where do I send the bill?"

Ms. Friendly Ad-Taker was more astute than our phone conversation would indicate, for my ad got an unbelievable response.

First, an insurance agent called and promised to work up a comprehensive retirement plan for whatever it was I was looking for once I found it.

Then an animal addict whose favorite pet had just thrown a new litter called to offer one which was nearly housebroken and could be easily trained to fetch my slippers.

Next, someone called to say that the neuron I was looking for was actually his elderly mother's. She'd lost it, he said, when she escaped from the nursing home he'd registered her into nineteen years ago so that she could have perpetual care.

[68]

If someone actually found it and answered my ad, he said, I need only give him a hint about how many carats it was and whether it was set in gold or platinum so that he could identify it and return it to his beloved escaped mother, when and if she returned to perpetual care, where they have TV in the day room.

As it turns out, I'm still looking for replacement neurons. And if you've read this far you can see that I need them badly.

If you have any, I will be happy to pay a good price for them. In fact, I would even trade a reasonable quantity—$.13 \times 10^7$ or so—for my knowledge of a particular fishing spot on the Popple River where a trophy brook trout, hook-jawed and colorful, weighing maybe six pounds, perhaps more, makes his home.

As I recall it, that fish is so hungry and ferocious that he will engorge any lure thrown at him the moment it hits the water.

But you'll need to send me the neurons first, you see, because without a mess of them to add to and replace the several Quads I've already lost to age, sun and martinis, it's unlikely that I'll ever remember precisely where that big trout lies.

An Evening on the Willow

Willow Creek flows through central Wisconsin not far from where naturalist Aldo Leopold was inspired to create the prophetic passages in his classic book *A Sand County Almanac*.

Golden-bottomed and vodka-clear, the slim and twisting Willow is a flyfisherman's frustration. For more often than not, when dabbling in this insubstantial water, the angler will use most of his allotted time to disengage his backcast from the grasp of streamside brush and he will use only a little of it in the pleasure of seeing his fly curl delicately into the window of a rising trout.

The Willow's bounties, too—unexpected hordes of wily brown trout—are angler-wary and skittish, making the stream something of a golden yoke for its regulars.

But many of the fish are of bragging size and they materialize in the frothy pools at dusk during the half-dozen mid-summer evenings when a nimbus of giant Green Drakes bursts off the placid water in a storm of translucent wings.

At such times, it's enlivening to be on the Willow although the constraints of small-stream flycasting in the slightly illuminated deceptiveness of moonlight seldom results in a heavy creel.

Yet, casting a feathered imitation here is exciting—a test of flyfishing skill. And some have likened the creeling of a Willow Creek brown trout to be the equivalent of running fifty straight in skeet or of being top rifle in Wyoming's One-Shot Antelope Hunt.

So it was with delight that I accepted a Saturday evening invitation to fish the height of the Willow's Green Drake hatch on a privately owned stretch of this infamous stream.

Indeed, I was elated.

But, on Friday, when I announced my good fortune to my wife, Carol, she spoke of different plans: "The lawn looks like a hayfield," she reminded me, ". . . the neighbors are complaining."

"If they loved nature," I responded, "they would recognize that our lush vegetation is beneficial to birds and to other natural creatures."

"Chipmunks, field mice, garter snakes . . . rats?"

"Them, too," I replied.

Typically, she ignored my astute reasoning and blurted on: "The weatherman is predicting rain for Sunday . . . If you don't mow the lawn tomorrow you know you won't get it done for another week.

"And that reminds me," she continued, "the roof still leaks where the ice pushed under the flashing on the eave last January."

"It's only a dribble," I protested, "and it's in the laundry room where nobody can see it."

But by now there was no stopping her: "I can't open the front door because it's warped from the humidity," she intoned. "And the front steps need repainting. When the paperboy comes to collect it's an embarrassment."

"The paper boy?"

"Yes," she said. "I have to tell him to walk around to the back door and he thinks . . . he *thinks* . . . you know."

"Hold on," I parried. "I showed you in that how-to book where it says never to paint in summer because the sun will cause the paint to blister. It's better to do the job in fall."

"Don't pull *that* on me," she bristled. "You know darn well that you'll spend all October hunting grouse and woodcock."

"September?"

"Salmon fishing on Lake Michigan."

"Early November?"

"Bow hunting for deer.

"Plus," she added, "you promised that we'd go out to dinner Saturday night."

"Oh?" I said, for this was the first I'd heard of it.

By now it was apparent that if I was to spend an evening on the Willow I'd need to take a different tack: I would need to do what one must do in all good marriages—compromise.

"O.K." I suggested, "I'll fish the Willow tomorrow evening and in return I will take you out to dinner *Sunday* evening. How's that?"

Surprisingly she agreed, and immediately proceeded to increase the tempo of our negotiations.

Minutes later I found myself consenting to: (1) mowing the lawn after work Monday; (2) painting the steps Tuesday; (3) patching the

[71]

roof Wednesday; (4) fixing the front door Thursday; (5) taking her to a disco Friday; and, (6) over the following weekend, tripping out of town to visit several of her relatives whom we hadn't seen since Christmas.

All in all, I figured it a pretty good arrangement—a reasonable compromise.

But when I recounted all this to a co-worker the following Monday, he looked disdainfully at me and commented: "Some compromise . . . It's a good thing you aren't the one who negotiates our labor contract."

"You must not be a flyfisherman," I replied.

"No," he agreed. "But how did you know?"

"If you were," I said, "you wouldn't needle me like that. You'd understand that I got the better of the deal."

"Oh," he said, interested now, "you caught lots of trout?"

"No," I answered. "I didn't creel a single one."

A Gentle Reminder

*T*he worst of the thundershower had passed and now the moist night air was heavy with the scent of wild rose and honeysuckle. Weary from a day of trout fishing on the Pine River at Jenning's Falls, Bill, Razzby, Terry, Paul and I huddled under the tent canopy to escape the rain. A bottle of Ernest and Julio Gallo's best chill-fighter promoted conversation. Halfway into it Razzby asked: "Do you believe in God?"

"I don't know," I replied. "Providence certainly didn't smile on me today. No fish."

"Maybe it's the exemplary life you lead," Paul commented.

"What do you mean?" I asked innocently, reaching to pour another measure of brandy into my stainless steel Sierra cup.

"For one thing," Paul replied, "anybody who drinks this stuff without ice or a chaser just has to be bad."

Perhaps our speculations about a deity had come about because of the awesome beauty of the place. Our campsite, perched high on a granite cliff overlooking the rippling water of the falls, was a setting of haunting natural grandeur. Upstream and down the river was pocketed with deep pools which were interspersed with gravel-bottomed riffles and wide, smoothwater runs. On the rocky face below, an icy spring bubbling from a crack in the ancient granite provided the sweetest of drinking water. Nearby, a dozen others like it cooled the river and made this stretch of water a perfect midsummer home for trout. Fish gathered here from throughout the river in the torrid days of mid-July and remained until early September. Then they dispersed to spawn.

"This place must have been put here by design," Terry said suddenly. "It must exist for a reason. It has to be more than a coincidence of nature."

"Yes," Bill said, "it's been put here by God . . . for people like us."

[73]

"Bull!" I responded. "This place is an accident. It is nothing more than an overmature mountain range that has been worn down to size by the glaciers. Earth itself is an accident. You and I are accidents."

"You don't believe?" Bill was disturbed.

"Oh, I believe, all right," I rattled on, driven by something I didn't quite understand. "But I believe that man is responsible for his own acts. God is us. Hell is right here on earth. Heaven is right here, too. Our actions dictate which we shall live in."

"That's existentialism," Paul scoffed. "It went out with Greenheart rods and gut leaders."

"What?"

"It's a school of ethical thought that holds human existence to be unexplainable. Existentialists believe that man is unique, the universe hostile to him, and that he alone is responsible for the consequences of his acts."

"Precisely," I said. "We've created God as a convenience. We use the concept to hedge our bets. So long as we've a God to forgive us, we can continue our obscene behavior without fear of damnation."

"I don't buy that," Bill countered. "You're overlooking the historic record. You've forgotten the miracles. How else can you explain Christ's ascension? Or his turning water into wine? Or his making manna for the multitudes from a basket of fish and bread? Man hasn't the ability to do that."

"Oh, no?" I replied. "Wasn't landing on the moon a miracle? And isn't giving new life to a person by a kidney transplant or a coronary bypass essentially resurrection? And what about the fact that the average American farmer grows enough food to feed more than fifty people? Those are miracles . . . man-made miracles. And they're greater deeds by far than any that have been attributed to the gods."

"It still seems to me," Terry said, a frown cutting deep lines into his forehead under a thick cowl of unruly cornsilk hair, "that there has to be something to life beyond this."

"What," I said blithely, extending my arms and sweeping them in a wide arc to emphasize the point, "can be better than this?"

"I believe that it's time to turn in," Razzby interrupted. "It's three hours to daybreak and the trout are waiting."

The weather changed just before dawn as a high pressure zone moved over the area. With the passing of the front and with the river rising from the previous day's rain, we had ideal fishing conditions. And the catch reflected them.

[74]

That morning, Terry brought in a limit, the smallest of which measured ten inches. Bill's catch included a bragging-sized brown; Paul's a colorful fourteen-inch native brook trout.

Strangely, I didn't fare as well. My creel hid a pair of just-legal hatchery trout.

"Have trouble landing them?" Paul gibed as he peeked into my basket. "I don't see gaff marks."

I grimaced.

"Don't be so tough on our non-believing friend," Bill admonished. "As I see it, he's already in big trouble. Those minnows could be a gentle reminder from the Man upstairs."

I didn't comment on Bill's words, nor could I bring myself to talk about a much larger fish I'd netted that morning, then quickly released—a robust river chub, dark red in color, which had bony protrusions on its head that resembled diminutive horns.

Grandma's Trout

*I*n summer, I sometimes make a pilgrimage to the tiny village of Wonewoc. There, in a whitewashed cottage high on a craggy bluff overlooking the deep and crooked valley in which the town is situated, I take time out from the world to commune with the spirits that are said to float about the nether. And, to spice the venture, I make dawn and evening flyfishing forays for the colorful native brook trout that are harbored in fair numbers by the icy waters of a nameless valley stream.

The cottage, although lacking the usual facilities one expects of vacation accommodations, is inexpensive, bright and airy; and its single French-paned window opens on a breathtaking vista of the valley, twisting through the mists far below.

Atop the bluff—my weekend aerie—a dozen cottages similar to mine encircle two long, low central buildings of frame construction, also whitewashed. One serves as a dining hall and the other as a chapel for the spiritualist sect that has used the encampment as a summer meditation place for more than thirty years.

No, a visitor need not be a member of the sect to spend a weekend here, all are welcome, even agnostics, such as I.

The spiritualists believe that certain of us have powers that allow communication with the spirits of those who have departed this life and have passed on to the next level of existence. These special people, many of them crones, wizened and wise, are called "mediums."

The mediums act as interpreters between those of us not blessed with the power and those in the spirit world with whom we wish to commune. The act of mediumship, if it takes place in a lighted place is called a "reading," and if in the dark a "seance."

One Saturday, after my early morning visit to the trout stream proved largely unproductive, and with nothing more to do until the evening hatch, I arranged for a meeting with a medium named

[76]

Madame Selma, a lady, I was told, of extraordinary powers, renowned even among her fellows in this restricted occupation.

Earlier, during a conversation with two of the encampment's repeat pilgrims, one suggested that I might learn something novel about myself if I were to join their devotions.

"Perhaps, I might," I replied, quickly interjecting the excuse that I was brought up in the Christian faith and therefore found it hard to believe in anything so nebulous as spirits, much less spirits that talked.

"Spiritualists are Christians, too," the other of the pair explained. "We believe in God and in Christ and in the tenets of the Bible."

"Yes," enjoined his companion, "and if you're a Christian you must believe in angels, right?"

"I suppose I do," I replied, suddenly realizing that his astute reasoning was about to entrap me.

". . . And if there are angels," my inquisitor went on, "wouldn't they be spirits? And if the angels are spirits, wouldn't they, under certain circumstances, have the capacity to be heard by living humans?"

Since I could not refute this logic without making myself out to be a hard-core nonbeliever, thus risking being barred from a pleasant place to stay during those times I fished the valley stream, I acceded to the reading.

Now, as I entered Madame Selma's cottage—where a fire burned briskly in an ancient pot-bellied wood stove despite the near-noon heat of a midsummer day—I actually looked forward to the experience. For I could recall no recent acquaintance who had passed into the spirit world. And I chortled to myself in sly anticipation: "That lack will surely put Madame Selma to the test."

Then, as I stepped through the door and hesitated a moment to adjust my vision to the dimness of the interior, a raspy voice crackled impatiently. "Come in. Come in. And close the door, please. These old bones don't take kindly to a draft. Arthritis, you know."

Madame Selma, dressed in a faded floral print house dress, was seated in a cane-backed rocker near the stove. She was gaunt and wrinkled, with a sharp nose and a long thin chin. Her silver hair had been recently done in quiet curls and washed in some preparation that had left it tinted with shades of an incredible iridescent blue, precisely mirroring the color of her eyes, which were alert and penetrating.

[77]

"You don't believe in this spirit business, do you sonny? I can tell," said Madame Selma, motioning with a gnarled forefinger that I should be seated on the only other chair in the room, a prim and rickety maple ladderback.

"I really don't know," I replied.

"They all say that at first," she said absently, closing her eyes and lapsing into what appeared to be some sort of trance.

I said nothing, and she rocked, eyes closed, her chin resting lightly on her chest. The only sounds in the room were the *creak, creak, creak* of her rocker and the occasional snap of wood burning in the stove. Outside, hidden in the listless leaves of the oaks, cicadas rasped and birds twittered here and there.

"I see an old woman," said Madame Selma suddenly. "She is shorter than me and much stouter. She speaks English with an accent. She is dressed in a thick wool sweater and wears heavy, high-topped shoes . . . the kind farmers wear. I see her shambling down a country road, climbing through a barbed-wire fence, and crossing a field of parched hay to reach a tiny home in need of repair. She carries a stout canvas bag on a strap over her shoulder . . . A young boy is playing in the sand near an apple tree in the yard . . . I believe that boy is *you!*"

"My God!" I said involuntarily. "Grandma Rebman! I haven't thought of her in years. She was a Polish immigrant who lived on a nearby farm. She died many years ago."

Madame Selma opened her eyes and smiled. "Would you like to speak with your old friend? Would you like to ask her a question? Yes, I think you would. And she will answer. Her spirit is coming to me very strong today."

"I suppose so," I responded. "But what shall I ask her?"

"Anything you wish," said Madame Selma.

I thought, but could think of nothing of merit to ask Grandma Rebman's spirit and finally I said, "Could you ask her if she knows where the trout are hiding in the valley stream? Or is that too frivolous? My luck hasn't been too good this weekend."

"Of course you may ask her," said Madame Selma, going on to explain: "But you must realize that you will not actually hear the voice of the spirit. Those voices can only be heard by a few fortunate and gifted persons such as myself. I hear what the spirit speaks and then translate it so that you will understand. I am merely the intermediary. It is my voice you will hear, but the spirit's words."

I nodded. Madame Selma closed her eyes and rocked.

[78]

After a moment, a strange, throaty voice, heavily accented in a language I recognized as Polish, came from Madame Selma's lips.

"Walt," I was startled when the voice addressed me because I had not told Madame Selma my name and she had not inquired of it, "you know that I wasn't much on fishing in my other life . . . I had too much work tending that parcel of sand dunes and quack grass we called a farm. And there wasn't much time for cavórting; not with those eight hungry kids to feed. But occasionally me and Grandpa would sneak off for some perch fishing on Green Bay . . . you know . . . at the mouth of the river. My lands, Grandpa and me had some times there, let me tell you. I remember the Saturday night we went skinny dipping in the moonlight and afterwards Grandpa . . ."

"Ah . . . Grandma Rebman," I coughed politely. "Can we get back to the trout?"

"You were always the impatient one," the voice said. "I remember that time you tried to set the record for strawberry picking. We paid you five cents a quart, remember? And that day you went for the record you brought in over one hundred quarts. But later, when we checked them before sending them to market, we found that you'd filled the bottom half of most of the boxes with gravel stones. Oh, you were a one."

"Grandma," I tried to draw her from her reminiscing, ". . . the trout?"

"My lands, forgive me for prattling on like this," the voice said. "But I don't get much of a chance to talk with anyone down there nowadays. Most of my old friends are up here, you know . . . Yes . . . The trout . . . Well, I don't know too much about trout but I saw a very large fish in that stream of yours just yesterday. It was shiny green on top with a white belly and had red and blue spots all along its sides."

"A brook trout," I interjected.

"Yes," the voice said. "I believe that's what it's called. This one was under the streambank where a large rock sticks out of the water. The rock is on the outside of a sharp bend just upstream of a small meadow."

"Yes," I burst out. "I know the place! Thank you, Grandma. Thank you."

"Think nothing of it. But please come back sometime soon and visit with me again."

"I will, Grandma," I said, itching to get to the stream and tackle the speckled beauty that I was already affectionately thinking of as "Grandma's Trout."

Madame Selma opened her eyes, rubbed them as if waking from a deep sleep in an unfamiliar motel room, not knowing exactly where she was, and looked about, dazed. "Well," she said. "Did the spirit speak?"

"You bet it did!" I replied.

"Are you satisfied with your reading?"

"Oh, yes. More than satisfied."

"That'll be ten dollars, then," Madame Selma said. "You can drop it into the candy dish on the table on your way out. And make sure you close the door. The arthritis, you know."

Ten dollars! I had only three five-dollar bills in my wallet plus some change in my pockets. But if Grandma's trout was where she said it was, the fee was worth it. I dropped two of the bills into the candy dish and quietly closed the door behind me before rushing to my car to make use of my newly acquired knowledge.

Grandma's trout was there all right, just where she said it would be. And the fish was indeed a trophy, more than twenty inches long and perhaps six pounds. But it would not accept any of my offerings.

I tried dry flies of every size and description, floating them delicately into its window without the hint of drag. Grandma's trout would merely nose them curiously before curling insolently away to return to its lair under the cutbank.

Then I tried streamers, wet flies and finally weighted nymphs. Nothing would entice Grandma's trout into striking.

At last, when the dying rays of the setting sun just touched the surface of the water, illuminating the stream with an ethereal luminescence of rare beauty, I tied on a huge, showy White Miller, a fly that had proved its worth as a twilight fish-taker many times before.

But Grandma's trout would have none of it, choosing instead to drown my sure-fire nighttime trout-killer with a mighty flip of its tail.

Long after dusk I quit the stream in frustration and went back to my cottage on the aerie to lapse into fitful sleep. And then, sometime between midnight and dawn, when eerie silver light from the full moon filtered through the French-paned window to strike my head as I tossed on the lumpy feather-filled pillow, the idea struck me: "Why not arrange another reading with Madame Selma early tomorrow and ask Grandma Rebman a second question—*What will the trout bite on?*"

The next morning, as early as propriety would allow, I knocked at Madame Selma's cottage door.

"Come in. Come in," she called irritably. "You don't have to break the door down. It isn't locked."

"Madame Selma," I said, as soon as I'd entered. "May I have another reading?"

"Ah," she said, "it's you. So you're a believer now, I see. And so early. What prompts that? No, let me answer *that* myself. You wish to commune again with Grandma Rebman so that you can ask her what that trout you're after is hungry for, right?"

"Yes," I agreed. "But there's one more thing."

"Oh? What's that?"

"Well . . ." I said, as delicately as I could, "I have only five dollars and some change . . . enough to buy my breakfast . . . left to my name. Could you give me a limited reading? Enough to ask Grandma Rebman that single question?"

"I might," said Madame Selma, "but I'd like to know what you will do with the words of the spirit once you have them?"

"Get Grandma's trout, what else?" I said flippantly, then hastily added, "and share it with you, of course."

"In that case, and seeing how you're short of funds, I'll give you a limited reading. I may be old but I remain a pragmatist, you see."

Madame Selma settled down into her creaking rocker, closed her eyes in the semblance of entering a trance, and soon two words, this time in perfect unaccented English, issued from her lips: *Use nightcrawlers.*

"Use nightcrawlers!" I exploded. "What kind of advice is that to give a flyfisherman?"

"Madame Selma opened her eyes, looked directly at me, and with just the proper touch of humor she said, "Sonny, what more can you expect for a lousy five bucks?"

A Questionable Decision

There was a time when my name was flagged "Hot Pros-pect" in the catalog department of all the sellers of mail order fishing gear.

I enjoyed this preferred status, of course, because it kept me well supplied with a basic angling necessity—wish books.

Unfortunately, the annual mailing of these dazzlingly illustrated modern art forms was timed to arrive in my mailbox shortly after New Year's Day. Usually, they were accompanied by unpaid Christmas bills and notices of taxes due.

So in my case, these offerings were petitions of futility. I yearned, but I could not respond with a paid-for order.

And after several Januarys of no orders the flow of preseason tackle catalogs slowed as the "Hot Prospect" tag was removed from my name.

Soon, the automatic mailings ended—reserved, I suspect, for buyers, not wishers.

So one weekend in February, when the snow was too crusted for cross-country skiing, I would sit down with a fistful of coins, a roll of postage stamps, and a pile of coupons gleaned from outdoor magazines to exhort the mail order people to speed my once-free fantasies to me.

And in that way, for a pittance, I maintained my dreams of one day owning the ultimate in a bamboo flyfishing rod and assortments of hackle hand-tied by Lee Wulff, Dave Whitlock, and other masters of insect deceit.

Promptly upon receipt of each catalog, I eagerly examined the new temptations and dutifully recorded which tackle I would send away for the moment I "came into money."

Although the task was agonizing, it was also perversely enjoyable. And I soon developed a sort of a love-hate attitude toward those far-away purveyors of my dreams.

[82]

But the ritual of wishing and circling, pondering and listing, had a dampening effect on my yearning and, when completed, I always felt contented for a while.

Still, I knew that within a few days, sometimes only within a few hours, I would re-examine my imaginary order to wonder to myself: "What possessed me to think I need an epoxy-coated backing splice from Orvis? The money might be better spent on a set of Dan Bailey's famous muddler minnows."

Thus, soon after an aspiration had hit my mind, the list would be revitalized to reflect a later passion.

Then, cheerfully, I savored my good fortune at having discovered my errors in time—before the windfall came and the money squandered on nonessentials.

Meanwhile, I flayed the waters of Wisconsin's Pine, Popple, Pike and Peshtigo rivers with an old, eight-foot, glass-fibre rod. The loose ferrule caused occasional problems, and the squeaky single-action reel had a broken handle made serviceable with a few winds of electrician's tape, but the make-do outfit took trout.

Still I imagined, when casting to a fine rise at thirty feet, what it would be like to lay out seventy feet with ease and to set a hook in the monster brown trout that always taunted me from the far side of Camp One Rapids Pool.

So over the years my dreams have not diminished. Indeed, they might even have improved. For example, I started out wishing for a good glass rod. That soon became a desire for one of the less expensive bamboo rods. And that desire was eventually replaced by a craving for computer-fitted, six-splice, epoxy-coated, Tonkin cane.

With such a rod I *knew* I could cast rhythmically for hours on end. The line would always turn a tight loop over a distant fish and drop a midge delicately on mirror-smooth water without spattering so much as one drop to spook the quarry.

Season after season, I dreamed on.

Then, a few weeks before Opening Day last year, good fortune! An unexpected windfall from a bonus at work. After taxes, my wife, Carol could replace the sagging livingroom sofa and there would be enough left to invest in the one thing I most cherished: The ultimate in a flyrod and reel.

But after all those years of chasing dreams, of learning nearly all there is to know about choosing the perfect flyfishing combination, I still had doubts!

[83]

A rod with two matched tips made sense. If one tip were to be broken accidentally, I'd have a replacement to use and a trip wouldn't be ruined.

But a two-tip rod meant there would only be enough of the bonus money left to buy an inexpensive single-action reel. And what my ultimate rod called for was an English-made, magnesium, no-post, two-to-one retrieve ratio, mulitplier reel strung with shooting head line of precise dimensions.

And what angler so equipped could select a fly from a recylced plastic box? Only a 24-compartment Wheatley would do.

Finally the agonizing decision: buy the finest rod, with only one tip; buy the finest reel, with only one spool; and buy the necessary accouterments with the savings.

Reasonable. Logical. But as it turned out, dead wrong.

On Opening Day, when I tried my ultimate assembly at streamside for the first time, there came a series of events that even now I recall only in brief flashes near incoherence:

A dozen casts to my favorite pool on the Popple River. One strike. Miss. No further action. Move on. A big, boiling rise off the tip of a huge, downed white cedar near Willow Pool. Clamber through the brush so I won't spook the fish. Sneak slowly along the slippery, moss-covered trunk. Slip. Fall. Feel the rod tip catch in the grotesque, snaggled branches. Snap! The gut-churning sound of splintering bamboo. The single tip! Costs $95 to fit and replace. And I don't have it!

One dream fulfilled creates upon itself another. And having

bought, my name is again flagged "Hot Prospect" in the catalog departments of all the sellers of mail order fishing gear.

Rodless once more, and penniless, I again dream on.

I've noticed, for example, those Space Age graphite rods. At one-third the price of choice bamboo, they sure look good.

Anyone looking for the butt section of a $300 Tonkin cane? Will sacrifice.

The Deadliest Lure

Axel Abelman was napping in the warm September sun when a sudden lakeward pull jerked his rod from under the large rock he'd used to anchor it.

"Fish on, Axel," I called from farther down the breakwater where I was casting metal spoons in a variety of colors, sizes and weights in a fruitless quest for a fall-run steelhead.

At my call, Axel's head bobbed but he was too drowsy to notice his rod being slowly pulled to the edge of the breakwater by the trout's lazy initial run. Then, momentarily, just as the rod was about to plummet into the pounding waves ten feet below, the reel handle caught in the cracked concrete.

"Fish on, Axel!" I shouted. This time my warning prodded him into action. He rolled onto his back, sort of jackknifed upward, arms outstretched, and bellywhopped in the general direction of the disappearing rod. Somehow, as it slid over the edge, he managed to clutch both hands around the reel. Then, suddenly wide awake and alert, he twisted into a sitting position and thrust both arms— hard—above his head, setting the hook.

"Some guys have all the luck," I complained. "Some guys even catch fish when they're zonked out."

"I told you that the lure's the thing," he gushed as he thumbed the level-wind to turn what appeared to be a stronger-than-average steelhead. "Spawn sacks are deadly this time of year."

"Still-fishing isn't my idea of hot action," I countered. "It's more fun my way—casting hardware."

"How's this for action?" Axel chortled as his fish made a sweeping run parallel to the breakwater, stripping nearly a hundred yards of line from the spool against the lightly set drag.

"I'll admit that the fish you have on represents one more strike than I've had today. O.K.?"

[86]

"It's more than a strike," Axel needled. "It's your supper."

"Don't flop it in the pan until you've got it in the net," I replied dourly.

Unlike humans, rainbow trout, or "steelhead" as the lake-run variety is called around the Great Lakes, have no aversion to abortion. In spring and fall, when steelhead return to tributary streams to spawn, they will feed voraciously on their own eggs. Many anglers, noting their quarry's self-destructing dining habits, go after them by still-fishing with spawn sacks.

To make these ovarian imitations, anglers mold thumbnail-sized globs of fresh spawn around a Number 2 treble hook and hold the eggs together by wrapping a piece of close-meshed netting or a square of nylon cut from ladies' hosiery around the mass. Then they tie it tightly with thread beneath the eye of the hook. When a heavy ball or slip sinker is attached to the line about eighteen inches ahead of the rig, the wrapped spawn will float just off bottom and will trick the cannibalistic steelhead into thinking it will soon be mouthing a tidbit of its own natural caviar.

The technique works well and more Great Lakes trout and salmon fall victim to it than to any other lure. But to anglers like me, afflicted with impatience since birth, the method is unexciting.

Still, being consistently bested by a hotshot angler like Axel who is always deprecating of your unproductive ways, is generally incentive enough to compromise your principles.

So that evening, I bartered a pair of toenail-ruined panty hose from a friend. And using spawn from Axel's freshly caught female steelhead, I clipped squares of nylon and fashioned a dozen spawn sacks. To my untutored eye, they appeared more than adequate.

However, the next morning, after an hour of fishing off the breakwater within a few yards of Axel, I had only a dozen soggy spawn sacks to show for my effort while he had two fine fish on his stringer, both males. One was a sleek six-pounder and the other was a full-bodied trophy that pulled the spring-loaded scale to over the fourteen-pound mark.

"I thought you said these spawn sacks were deadly," I chided.

"Well . . ." Axel replied sheepishly, "I wasn't going to tell you, but steelhead won't bite on spawn tied in that brown-colored nylon you're using. White nurse's stockings are best."

"White nurse's stockings?"

"Yes," Axel confided. "And I'll let you in on something else: the

[87]

secret is to only use fabric from the top two inches of *thigh-length* white nurse's hose. Let me tell you, it's the deadliest lure."

"Where do you get something like that?" I inquired innocently.

"Sonny," he said, "if you need an old geezer like me to explain that, you'd better take up golf. You'll never make a steelhead fisherman."

The Return of the Viking

Sometimes, when I am aboard a Great Lakes charter fishing boat, I look toward the coastline which from this distance appears wild and uninhabited and imagine myself a Viking—I am of that ancestry.

"The sea is up," I hear the charter captain say. "If we're to catch some fish today we'll need to troll in the lee of Lighthouse Point."

"Sounds good," I absently agree, for the cloud shadows playing against the ruddy rays of the rising sun have formed the silhouette of a Viking ship which appears to ride the waves just this side of the horizon.

The Vikings—those robust progenitors of mine—sailed these very waters in the year 1000, several centuries before some wandering Frenchman named Nicolet was officially credited with their discovery in 1634. Skilled and daring seaman, the Norseman had journeyed across four thousand miles of uncharted sea to leave a runestone on a Lake Superior beach as evidence of their adventure.

Now, as I look eastward into the early morning light, I sense the Viking's presence here. The feeling is so strong I can form the cloud shadows into a three-dimensional Viking ship, high prowed with a single, square sail rigged amidships, speeding before the wind to its rendezvous with destiny.

And when I squint my eyes to telescope my vision, I believe I see standing before the single mast someone who could have been my great-grandfather several times removed. A sturdy man, he wears a horned metal helmet and braces himself against the pitching sea by using his bronze-tipped lance as a staff.

Then, as I watch intently, he lifts a curved horn trumpet to his mouth and sounds a strange and forlorn call.

"Hear that?" the charter captain interrupts my reverie. "Fog on the mainland. Perhaps we should head home."

[89]

"Not yet," I reply, still engrossed in my vision of the Viking.

Why had the Nordics come? Where were they going? What were they searching for?

One authority suggests that they sailed from the coast of Scandinavia to escape exploding populations and political restrictions in their homeland.

Another expert speculates that a slight warming of the climate once melted areas of polar ice. The melt cooled the northern seas, moving the Viking's favorite foodfish—cod and salmon—into the warmer ocean currents far offshore. The Vikings simply followed their food supply, discovered Iceland, then Greenland, then Vinland—the eastern seaboard of North America—and from what is now Flower's Cove, Newfoundland, their adventurous nature lured them to explore the Great Lakes waterway.

Whatever the reason for their journey to the New World's inland seas, today a certain empathy exists between us which somehow spans our separation of a thousand years.

Still, strangely, I react to the perceived presence of my Nordic forebears by feeling melancholy. Perhaps exploding populations, restrictive politics, and lack of fishing opportunity are crowding my spirit, too.

But unlike the Vikings, I cannot escape. The world's frontiers have all been breached by now. Through television and movies, most of the earth's exotic, faraway places have become so familiar to me that there's no thrill in visiting them. And thanks to the space probes which, appropriately enough, are a technological spin-off from the *Viking* rocket program of the early 1950's, I am as acquainted with the surface of the moon and the planet Mars as I am with my neighbor's backyard.

Each year, too, it becomes harder to elude the duress of consorting with the crowded earth outdoors even for a weekend.

Last opening day of fishing season, for example, we canoed the Popple River upstream to our traditional trout fishing campsite on secluded Camp One Rapids Pool. We'd had it to ourselves the first weekend in May for more than twenty years and we looked forward to the occasion as our annual bust-out from winter. But this opening day it was occupied by aliens who preferred nude swimming and boisterous partying to quiet angling.

Then, in July, we backpacked a half-dozen miles to a lakeside campsite in an area designated wilderness. The site, under a majestic grove of towering virgin hemlock, was a place of reverence and we'd escaped here many times. But this trip our stay was marred by some turkey named Mike who had carved his name in foot-high letters into the two-inch bark of the grandest tree.

His urge, of course, was prompted by that innate proclivity of mankind which causes travelers to leave their unsightly spore in every footstep. It is the same peculiarity which induced the Vikings to leave the runestone on a Great Lakes shoreline. But they, at least, had the good sense not to engrave the symbols of their passing in a living thing.

Now, behind me, the radio crackles. A voice identifies the caller as the skipper of the charter boat *Lucky Lady II*. He reports his party of six is trolling the lee of Lighthouse Point.

"The fog is building here," his voice intones, "and we haven't marked a fish in the past two hours. We're heading in."

"Hear that?" my charter captain speaks.

I nod.

"Let's hang it up."

"You're the skipper," I reply.

The captain settles into his seat on the flying bridge, tugs the visor of his cap to set it firmly on his head, twists the wheel to fix his craft on the compass heading to the harbor, and pulls the throttle back.

The boat surges forward, planes, and slaps the chop toward the onshore fogbank.

I swivel in my fishing chair to get a better view. The fog is rolling on the coast but out here the sky is bright and gold and clear and the angle of the sun has washed out all the early morning shadows.

As the boat drones on, I feel the wind in my hair, the cold spray off the bow stings my cheeks, and I catch the faint scent of pine from the nearest landfall. I am content.

But more exhilarating is the feeling I have of traveling into the unknown. For the fog obscures the coastline and I have no idea of where we are nor where we're going.

I stand, fix my gaze across the heaving bow toward the shrouded world ahead. And, legs widespread, I brace myself on a long-handled boat hook, its point gouged into the deck against the pitching sea. The foghorn sounds its strange and forlorn call. For the moment, at least, the Viking has returned.

Escape from Skull Cave

Along a certain limestone cliff that creates one side of a creek valley somewhere in the Northwoods, there is a narrow opening to a passageway in the rifted rock that follows a fissure to a cavern deep underground. I was down there once, with Leonard White Deer, an Ojibway Indian friend since childhood. We were searching for the huge trout, many of trophy size, that congregate in the cavern pool during the hottest days of midsummer. Once, I had one on, a giant of a brook trout, but since our escape, I have never wished to visit there again.

It began rather innocuously one firey August day when Lenny and I were flailing the sluggish waters of the Pine River in a fruitless quest for a rising trout.

"I wonder where the big trout go this time of year?" I muttered sullenly as I cast into the eddy below Big Bull Falls, Class 1 trout water that produced good-sized fish early and late in the season but appeared to be barren now.

"They're in the cooler water of the tributary streams," said Lenny. "Everyone knows *that!*"

"Oh, yeah," I replied. "During the past two weeks I've explored every trickle of water that comes into this so-called trout stream and the only place I rolled a fish is where Disappearing Creek goes underground."

"You trespassed on reservation lands?" said Lenny, nervously fingering his heavy, bearclaw necklace. "It's a good thing the tribal police didn't catch you. Worse, the place where Disappearing Creek goes underground is considered sacred. No ordinary Ojibway will go near it—only the *Midewewin*, the medicine men. And the agents from the Federal Bureau have since declared it off limits even to those shamans.

[92]

"Why is it sacred?" I wanted to know.

"It's said to be the place of *Herok'a,* earth spirits that have been infused with *Herecgunina,* the power of evil. And there are stories about tribal hunters who inadvertently wandered into the area, never to return. But the real reason the local federal bureaucrats have declared it off limits is something else."

"Oh? What's that?"

"The bastards administrating this reservation are all greedy and corrupt!" replied Lenny vehemently. "I suspect they want to keep the location of potential archeological sites secret so they can strip them of artifacts at their leisure. Then, they can sell the treasures to private collectors for big prices and head back to the city with fat bank accounts. I wish there was a way to get rid of the lot of them."

"What has that to do with our going there for trout?"

"The agents consider me a troublemaker," said Lenny, smiling. "And they've threatened to cut the tribe's federal funding if the council doesn't keep me and some of the other young braves in line. It's bureaucratic blackmail, pure and simple. But I got the word not to hassle them . . . or else."

"Or else?"

"Yeah . . . or else. Some of the chiefs and the sub-chiefs are skimming the federal funds—taking action off the top; salting it away. They're tough and enjoy living the good life . . . sort of an Indian mafia. And there's a lot of timber on the reservation in which to hide bodies."

"But if the creek does flow from some hidden underground cavern," I goaded, "that could be where the big trout go in summer. Think of those huge, hook-jawed beauties, Lenny. They'll all be gathered in one place . . . a real Glory Hole—like a Northwood's elephant graveyard, except our Eldorado will be loaded with hungry, *living* trout. Let's give it a try."

"I didn't say I wouldn't go," said Lenny, brushing back his silken blue-black hair from a broad forehead the color of burnished copper. "I was merely pointing out the risks. To hell with them all. We'll take off early tomorrow morning. Meet me on the back road near the place where we go blueberry picking. It's off the reservation so no one will see us leave."

Today, looking at the scar on my right forearm, and thinking of the sinister events that followed and continue to this day, I wish Lenny White Deer hadn't been so easy to convince. At the time, I thought he agreed simply because he was as addicted to trout fishing as I was. But that, of course, was before our escape from Skull Cave.

The next morning, after stuffing our fishing gear and a light lunch into our backpacks and donning hip boots, it didn't take long to find the entryway to the underground cavern. Indeed, finding it was almost too easy. And I have the feeling that Lenny knew precisely what he was about and had somehow tricked me into going along as a back-up man, in the event of trouble. I suspect, too, that he knew a white outsider would not relate the details of the adventure to other members of the tribe. And now that I think of it, perhaps it was the reason for his telling me the part about the Indian mafia.

We followed the creek upstream from its mouth to where it disappeared underground in a tiny sedge meadow rung with alders and cedar. Here and there, huge blocks of the brownish-gray limestone had fallen to form jumbled masses of talus at the base of the cliff. The rock face was perpendicular, rising upwards more than a hundred feet and devoid of vegetation. The rocks were formed more than 350 million years ago from calcium that precipitated out of an ancient sea that covered the area. The shells of billions of small sea animals that had died and sunk to the bottom built up other layers and added weight. Later, during a period of earthquakes, this part of the land fractured and was pushed up along a geologic fault, forming the cliff. And this type of limestone, I knew, as did Lenny, was weak and easily dissolved by underground water. It was stone that wasn't really stone, more like rock candy. Water moving through it over thousands of years would form channels, ducts, tunnels and corridors, even caves and caverns and underground rooms . . . That is what we hoped to find, somewhere under the valley of Disappearing Creek.

I had explored no more than a half-dozen holes and clefts, none deeper than a few feet, when Lenny called: "I've found it . . . over here."

He was standing atop a gigantic disarray of fallen rock that screened an opening in the cliff face about the size of a casement window. Around the hole, a series of barely discernible pictographs—oval shapes surrounding intricate designs of faded blue and red—indicated that others had been there in some far off time.

"What do the symbols mean, Lenny?"

"I don't know," he said. "They're too deteriorated to read. But the

[94]

fact that they're here means this is no ordinary tunnel. It must lead somewhere."

"Of course," I said confidently, "it leads to the fish. And incidentally, how did you know what you found?"

"What?"

"When you called you said, 'I've found it.' How did you know what it was?"

"Just a feeling I had," he said, "a sudden feeling."

As a precaution, we'd each brought a powerful five-cell flashlight equipped with new long-life batteries. And Lenny had a large roll of heavy twine, the kind masons and carpenters use. We planned to lay it behind us so that we would have something to lead us back in the event we became disoriented underground. Now, Lenny tied the loose end of the roll to a fencepost-sized block of limestone in the talus outside the opening and gestured expansively. "After you," he said. "I'll tend the line."

I saluted, bowed and pushed the flashlight switch, then squatted to wiggle through the narrow entryway.

Immediately, even before I felt the cool, moist air welling up from the depths, I was struck by a strangely familiar odor that I couldn't quite identify. It was a sweetish, musky smell, similar to that of putrefying apples. I was sure that I'd smelled something like it before but where, or to what it could be attributed, I could not recall.

A few dozen steps later, the passageway narrowed, funnel-like, and I dropped to all fours and was forced to cock my shoulders as I crawled forward. Lenny, who was bulkier than me, grunted and puffed as he struggled along behind.

"If this project produces trout," I said, "we'll have the place all to ourselves. Nobody but a trout fisherman or some fool spelunker would get himself into a mess like this."

"Maybe . . ." Lenny started to say, allowing the remainder of his remark to trail off.

"Maybe what?"

"Not maybe *what*," Lenny responded absently. "Maybe *who*."

Soon, the passageway sloped steeply downward. Then it angled sharply to the right. I jackknifed my body at the waist to twist around the corner and the beam from my flashlight pierced a hollow blackness beyond. "It's a cave," I announced, pulling myself through. "This might be the pool."

A quick survey with the lights showed no water, only a sandy-

[95]

floored oblong cave, about the size of an ordinary ranch house. I ran the light over the walls, pocked with nooks, crannies and alcoves; then along the floor to the far end where I let it rest on several piles of what appeared to be trash. "Shit, Lenny," I fumed. "The cavers have beaten us. And they've left their lousy garbage for someone else to carry out."

"No," Lenny said sharply, "that isn't garbage. Don't you call that garbage!"

I should have recognized Lenny's outburst as a sign of something sinister. I see that now, but at the time it made no more than a momentary impression because I saw, too, that the piles were really heaps of bones and artifacts—dusty, yellowed with age, obviously very, very old.

Most interesting was a circle of large ovoid skulls, of the same shape as the pictographs outside the entryway, and painted in the same, intricate red and blue design. They had been arranged so that all the muzzles pointed inboard, toward the center of the circle.

"What do you make of these, Lenny?"

"Bear," he said tersely, "awaiting the resurrection. This must be the meeting place of the Bear Cult."

"The Bear Cult?"

"Yes, according to the stories my grandfather told me, it was a secret society of fierce Ojibway warriors who always took the lead in forays against our enemies. Not much is known about them, but see how those piles of bones are mounded behind each skull? The ancient Ojibways believed that if the bones of an animal were preserved, in the course of time they would be replenished with flesh. Then the lost spirits could re-enter the new body and the animal would come to life again."

"I *knew* that odor was familiar," I said. "It's the scent of bear. The stink in this cave is exactly the same odor I smelled when I came across a hibernating bear while snowshoe hare hunting last winter. The bear was in a hole under the roots of an old blowdown. You could smell him from a half-block away."

"You noticed the smell, too?" said Lenny, frowning. "I didn't know if you had so I didn't mention it. Anyway, whatever it is we're smelling isn't coming off these old bones."

He stooped to pick up a small metal object and handed it to me. "If the bones are the same age as this copper gouge, they've been here for a few thousand years. This tool dates from the time of the old

Copper Culture Indians. They lived in this area three thousand years before the time of your Christ."

"Hell, Lenny," I said blithely. "You don't have to get personal about this. Besides, you know I'm an agnostic."

Ordinarily, Lenny would have come back at my remark with some witty repartee. And that, too, should have warned me. But I didn't notice his oversight; things were happening too fast.

Skull Cave was a treasure trove of Indian artifacts. There were birch bark scrolls etched with pictographs that fell apart at our touch; pottery and baskets; and piles of axeheads, spearpoints and arrowheads, some still attached to remnants of feathered, wooden shafts.

But the most interesting objects were an exquisitely formed club and the grotesque wooden effigy of a bear with a massive head and limbs too small for the size of its body. The effigy, too, had a tiny, flint-tipped arrow run through its chest in the location of the heart.

Squatting, Lenny picked up the club. It was beautifully formed of a dark, lustrous wood, possibly walnut. The design was elegantly simple: a heavy business end shaped in the representation of a human head. The head tapered to form a handle that resembled a leg ending in a curved, crippled foot. And along its length the club was inlaid with bands of shell.

"If I remember my college archeology," Lenny said, "this is priceless. It's what's known as a ball-headed club, one of an Ojibway warrior's most prized possessions. The inlay work is called *wampumpeak.*"

"And the wooden bear," I queried, "why the distortion? Why the arrow through its heart?"

"The wooden effigies of the Ojibway were made for much the same reason that the voodoo dolls are still made in the Caribbean Islands today," said Lenny. "If you desired to do evil to something, you made an image of it and ran it through the heart with an arrow or a quill."

"That means," I said, "that the cult warriors who assembled here in Skull Cave didn't come to worship the bear, but came to destroy it."

"No!" said Lenny, "that isn't the way it is at all. We respect the bear. We have reverence for it. We don't fear it nor do we wish to destroy it. This bear was a rogue. Notice how we carved this effigy;

[97]

it's distorted. This bear was not a real bear but a mutant. It ravaged my tribe. It killed; ate our babies. That's why we must destroy it."

His outburst startled me. I looked at him, saw his eyes glaze over. It was as if he were in another time, far from the present, yet still here with me—here in Skull Cave.

"Lenny," I said, grasping his shoulders and shaking him, "do you know where you are? Do you know whom you're with? Look at me!"

"Whatever are you carrying on about?" he asked, rocking his head and turning to avoid looking into my inquiring eyes.

"Lenny," I said. "Do you realize that you spoke of the Bear Cult in the present tense? You said, 'We don't fear it.' Does the Bear Cult still exist? Is that why you brought me here, as an expendable companion in the rediscovery of your shrine?"

"Did I say that?" Lenny responded glibly. "It must have been a slip of the tongue. As I told you, this stuff is thousands of years old. The Bear Cult died out long ago. Now let's see what we can do about finding that underground pool. I'm hungry for a meal of trout."

Then Lenny turned away from me, toward the circle of skulls, and I heard him chanting softly. I believe he said, as nearly as I can recall: "Oh Great Brother Bear, I have spread my dreams beneath your feet . . . tred softly lest you scatter the dust outward to the winds."

"What's that?" I asked.

"Nothing," he replied, and I saw his eyes again glaze over. "Just a bit of Ojibway poetry taught me by my grandfather. Strange that I should remember it now."

"Was your grandfather of the Bear Cult?"

Lenny looked at me, surprised. "I don't know," he said. "I really don't know."

As we searched for the passageway that would take us to the pool in the underground cavern where the Pine River trout might be waiting out the heat of summer, Lenny's absentmindedness disappeared and we found a slit in the far wall, tucked away in an alcove of rock beyond the circle of skulls. Cooler air, and that sweetish, musky odor, heavier than it had been before, wafted through the opening. Lenny sniffed. "This must be it," he said.

Unlike the cramped tunnel that had brought us to Skull Cave, the passageway we entered now was a man-sized corridor. We didn't need to stoop and it was wide enough to allow us to travel through at a brisk pace. But as soon as we entered, the sweetish, musky smell grew heavier and then became oppressive as the passage—several minutes of steady walking beyond the exit of Skull Cave—became a slot that we had to wiggle through on our bellies.

"God!" Lenny said. "That bear smell is worse than ever."

"A bear couldn't get in here," I said. "It's too narrow to admit anything much broader than a small cub. Besides, if a cub did get this far, and if he's making the stink, we would have seen its tracks on the sand back in the Skull Cave. And we didn't."

"Maybe," said Lenny. "But let's be careful. I've got a queasy feeling. Something I can't control. This place is giving me the creeps. It's as if something wants me to be here and wants to get inside me."

I laughed and said, "It's those spooky bear skulls. They're preying on your superstitions. That and this unholy smell."

The constriction of the passageway ran on for no more than a dozen yards, then it widened, both up and out, and we heard the sound of gurgling water.

"Hear that?" I said. "We're right on target."

But neither of us mentioned that the stench of decay had now become so onerous that it was agonizing even to breathe.

After the constriction of the slot the tunnel became a cavern. Multicolored stalactites hung from the ceiling high above, beyond the range of the flashlight beams. Some were as large as tree trunks and quite beautiful, in an eerie sort of way.

We walked toward the water sound and soon the light was reflected off the surface of a large pool, about the size of a football field end zone. The water was crystal clear, ten feet deep in places, with a bubbling current moving through it.

Then, still several yards away, we paused to admire what we'd found. It was satisfying. And then we saw them, hugging bottom, a tremendous school of trout—brook trout and brown trout—some of the largest I've seen outside a hatchery.

"Let's break out those rods," I said excitedly.

Quickly, I jointed my rod and snapped on a Number 2 gold *Mepps* spinner, my favorite big-trout lure. Then carefully, so I wouldn't spook it, I cast over the largest brook trout. It was finning, slowly, snout upstream, just off the sterile rocky bottom in midpool.

The spinner ran up and out, plopped lightly on the surface, well beyond my chosen fish. I slowly counted *ten*, allowing it to sink, then began my retrieve.

At the first flash of gold from the spinner blade when the lure twitched off the bottom, catching the light, my trout arched upward and sped toward the lure, slamming it hard and hooking itself deeply. But to be on the safe side, I brought the rod tip up sharply to set the hook. And as I did so I heard a loud splash from somewhere to my right.

"What the hell kind of lure are you using, Lenny?" I said, laughing and glancing over my shoulder. "A musky spoon? These trout are big; but not *that* big."

"I don't even have my rod broken out," he croaked.

And then the smell hit us, the oppressive gagging smell of rotting flesh blended with another odor so overwhelming that I retched. The slobber welled from my throat and out of my mouth to dribble over my chest and into the crystal water of the pool. There a dozen of the languid trout swept to engorge the foul stuff before it was swept away by the current.

I retched again, a dry and hacking choke. My cough was echoed, somewhere out in the darkness, by a low-pitched mewing sound interspersed with the *thunk* and *swish* of something very large and soft lurching toward us over the rocky floor. I jammed the rod under my foot where the fish could play against the lightly set drag and turned the flashlight toward the sound.

"Jesus Christ!" Lenny gasped.

The creature that was hunching toward us had the shape of a bear, but with the oversized head and the distorted, foreshortened legs we'd seen depicted in the wooden effigy of Skull Cave. Its head was weaving from side-to-side, muzzle tilted upward, apparently trying to seek us out by sense of smell. Chunks of what appeared to be fish flesh hung off its jaws and yellow foam, flecked with blood, bubbled from its nostrils and its mouth. It was as broad as the box of a pick-up truck and had it been standing upright, rather than lunging along on its belly, handicapped by its too-short limbs, it might have been twelve feet tall. Then we saw the eyes, terrible, unseeing eyes, glazed over with a grayish, gelatinous film.

As we stood mesmerized, watching the beast move sluggishly toward us, its snout testing the air, seeking us out, there were other similar sounds moving about the darkness beyond the range of the flashlight beams, closing in. I swept the light and found that we had been encircled by the creatures, perhaps eight of them, of different sizes, but all with the same distorted bear-like shape. It was as if we were being stalked by a swarm of giant, loathesome caterpillars.

"It's an entire family," I whispered. "A clan! That's what the symbols and the effigy were warning us about. They must have mutated and lived down here for the past three thousand years. Let's get the hell out of here. Where's the line?"

Then something happened to Lenny. He looked at me blindly, his eyes bulging madly from his head; his body spasmed, and his hands became grasping claws. "No!" he croaked, "not mutants . . . the souls of my Bear Cult brothers looking for a blood sacrifice. They want me . . . they want my soul!" Lenny was screaming now, frenzied, his glassified eyes not focusing—like a madman, as if possessed.

I grabbed him by the shirt and chopped the edge of my hand down hard on the base of his neck. He stumbled against me and I fell heavily to the rock-strewn floor, a sharp piece of cherty stone gashing my forearm. But I didn't feel the pain; for the animals, or whatever they were, perhaps scenting my blood and wishing to be the first to engulf their prey, began tearing at each other with their massive jaws. The momentary distraction left a gap in their ranks and in the light I saw the ball of twine laying on the floor beyond a pair of the smaller beasts.

Fortunately, the creatures were slow moving and I dragged Lenny over to the line and started to follow it back to the tunnel. Lenny, although somewhat recovered from the blow I'd used to quiet him, was still dazed and incoherent. I misjudged the speed of the smaller creatures, too. As they sensed that we would get away they whirled and lurched after us. I pushed Lenny toward the tunnel, the hot, stinking breath of the creatures close behind. Finally, as we entered the slot, which was too constricting to allow them entry, the creatures wedged themselves between the unyielding rock walls, whimpering like kittens who hadn't been fed, clawing and gnashing.

Lenny was docile now, but lacking full control of his muscles. His head lolled on his shoulders as I led him through Skull Cave and then pushed and prodded him through the confining passageway beyond. The fresh air soon revived him.

"What happened in there?"

"I think you were possessed," I said, explaining his weird behavior.

"That's absurd," he replied, rational and apparently normal once more.

"Maybe," I said. "But I think we should close off the entrance to the cave so no one else will find it."

[101]

"No!" Lenny's eyes took on much the same crazed appearance as they had when the bear-like creatures confronted us in the cavern. "I want it left open. I've a use for it."

Lenny and I never again talked about our experience nor have I asked him why he was so insistent that the cave entry remain open. Today, I sometimes wonder if our adventure really happened; perhaps I dreamed it. But I know that's not the case. I still have the ancient copper gouge that I dropped into my pocket after Lenny handed it to me that day in Skull Cave.

Lenny and I remain good friends; we hunt and fish together and I often visit him on the reservation. He's calmer now, more content and peaceable. Indeed, he is even friendly toward the two remaining federal agents. The other three, I've heard, have mysteriously disappeared since the summer we visited the cavern. But the authorities, I understand, are keeping the disappearances under wraps, not wishing to disrupt the routine of the reservation now that Lenny has returned to normal.

I don't know if this has any bearing on Lenny's recent complacency: but a day or two before each of the agents disappeared I saw Lenny give the unfortunate man a battered birch bark scroll. When I asked him what it was, he merely smiled and said, "A map of the places they might find artifacts to sell to their rich collector friends. They've promised me a commission on everything they sell."

Then, earlier today, after we learned that Washington is sending a team of investigators to trace the missing agents, Lenny invited me to go fishing. Since we were to fish a reservation trout stream that is normally off limits to outsiders, I was, of course, eager to go.

But Lenny didn't seem to have his mind on catching trout. He spent most of his time filling his creel with birch bark, the oldest, scruffiest specimens he could find.

Christmas Cardinal

*F*resh snow sugar-coated the spruce boughs in the wood across the country road and the bells in the village churchtower chimed across the miles to drift Christmas music over the farm.

Underfoot, the snow squeaked with the cold and, overhead, thousands of stars sparkled—chains of diamonds in a clear luminous sky.

On a night like this in 1848, perhaps, composer Edmund Sears had received the inspiration to write *It Came Upon a Midnight Clear*, the enchantingly lyrical carol the bells were playing now. Although I'd heard it many times, tonight I understood its meaning for the first time.

It was Christmas Eve, a time for sharing. And as I listened to the melody from the bells I molded a ball of venison suet, covered it with dabs of peanut butter, and impressed into it salted sunflower seeds—my gift to the Christmas cardinal.

The bird, for as long as I could remember at least, always appeared in our apple tree on Christmas morning. *Cheer, cheer, cheer*, it called, adding its voice to the happiness of the season.

Earlier, with the first snow of mid-November, the blue jays, chickadees and juncos had settled into the barren branches of the apple tree and watching their antics was delightful.

But the arrival of the cardinal, a fiery splash of scarlet against the arctic white, was a truer joy. His presence hinted of a mellower time, promised a genial future and, best of all, confirmed that Christmas, indeed, had come.

Now, as I pushed through the drifted snow to place the cardinal's Christmas breakfast, I noted that the day had suddenly grown colder. But I gave no more than a passing thought to the icy aura that was gathering now around the edges of the moon.

Only later, when I was awakened sometime after midnight by the harshness of the cold seeping through our sawdust-insulated farmhouse walls, did I recognize the meaning of the haze which had earlier begun to shroud the moon—it portended a massive storm, a real Northwoods blizzard. And its fury was erupting now!

I shivered through the night, awaiting morning, but the shrieking wind did not subside. *How, I thought, can Santa and his reindeer possibly make it through the bluster of this night to reach the Sandberg household?*

Then, later, I tossed and turned at a more foreboding thought: *What would happen to the Christmas cardinal?*

Impatiently, when first light filtered through the window, I wetted a finger and rubbed a peephole into the frosted glaze and looked toward the apple tree.

I saw that the wind-driven snow had mounded tightly around its trunk, nearly to the lowest branches. And the suet ball had been torn away, the length of bailer twine with which I'd tied it was frayed and whipping now straight-out before the wind.

I searched the area of the tree through the fierce intensity of the storm but I saw no sign of the Christmas cardinal.

Despondent, I was about to turn away when I thought I saw a movement in the lee of the trunk where the wind had swirled an igloo-like pocket into the drift.

Was *that* a flutter of red?

Excitedly, I quickly dressed and fought the storm toward the tree. It was the cardinal!

His feathers were encrusted with the driven snow. He could not fly. Then I felt the slight fluttering of his heartbeat quavering through my mittens into my hands. He was alive . . . but barely.

I carried him into the house where I wrapped him in a fluffy towel. And then I placed him, gently, near the woodbox behind the stove.

Later, as the bird responded to the warmth, the wind lessened . . . Gradually the storm subsided . . . And the snow stopped.

So by the time the cardinal had revived, the sky was shimmering brightly—a cold, steel blue—and the world outside was strangely quiet, blanketed in purest white.

I opened the kitchen door. And the cardinal, seeing freedom just beyond, cocked his crested head, fluffed his scarlet feathers, marched purposefully across the worn linoleum floor, and flew to his favorite perch in the highest branch of the barren apple tree.

Cheer, cheer, cheer, he called happily in well-timed innocence.

The Sandberg household gathered in the doorway and beamed at him with a similar joy!

Christmas had come.

PART II

. . . to the upland fields and forests

A Promise on the Wind

*H*ear it now, that whispering? Through the pinetops, through the marsh grass, through the cornflowers on the prairie, spraying now in sparkles off the Great Lakes surf. Hear it?

Any who have ever heard that whispering have come to know it well. It is the outdoors calling; the sum and substance of the outdoor experience—all one needs to know.

I love that sound. I love the *feeling* of that sound. Perhaps you do, too. For there's a promise carried on it.

And if you're like me, the lingering memory of that whispering is often all that fills the game bag or the creel. There is no protein in it to energize a body exhausted in pursuing it, but it becomes, somehow, admirable fare for a cluttered mind.

Consider, for example, that although I am a hunter I seem not to be a fortunate one. The greenhead mallards always flare from the impropriety of my calling to broadside over the blind on the other side of the lake. And the giant Canada geese, when I'm around, always orbit southward at stratospheric altitudes.

If I choose to hunt more earthbound creatures, such as ruffed grouse, the silvertails always boom away well before my self-trained Brittany chances to explore the covert, ever disdainful of my commands.

On a deer stand, the trophy buck I covet always elects to scratch his antlers on the brush which composes the blind I sat in yesterday. But tomorrow, the lout will travel to his evening dinner by prancing across my footprints of the day before.

Grey squirrels never peek around a tree at me and the coats of snowshoe hare turn invisibly white at the first hint of snow, which somehow happens to be the only chance I will have to hunt the hares for the season.

And whenever I attempt to show an outdoor novice how expert I

am at living off the land, the first identifiable plant we stumble into is poison ivy.

I fish, too, but I don't seem to be much of a fisherman! No matter how early I set my alarm, I always miss the spawning run by a full day or hit a "can't miss" blue-ribbon trout stream after the hatch when spentwing naturals are foaming in the vortex of every eddy and I have only a meager selection of Orvis weighted nymphs in my fly box.

Once, however, I was lucky enough to be thigh-deep in Willow Creek when the Green Drakes rose like fluff from a punctured feather pillow. But (you guessed it!) I was fishing ultra-light *spinning* tackle and my long-saved-for bamboo fly rod was reposing in a closet sixty miles away.

I'm a camper, too. But even that most innocuous of pastimes is a tribute to my ineffectuality:

My foil-wrapped potatoes always turn to charcoal in the campfire and my "indestructible" tent always blows down in the mildest zephyr, usually at 3 A.M.—but only when it's raining.

Canoeist? I'm that, too. But somehow my foam-supported "un-sinkable" craft always broaches on the slimmest sliver of midstream rock and I never get the thrill of a white-water ride because I must wade such exhilarating water pulling my sodden craft behind me.

Indeed, after twenty years of getting into the outdoors at the slightest opportunity to escape such mundane, unnecessary tasks as painting a scaly house, mowing a lawn so overgrown it could be used to train white hunters in pathfinding, or shoveling Snowstorm Cal out of the driveway, the only outdoor prowess I can claim is that I've undoubtedly missed more bonafide doubles on grouse than any other uplander, including red fox and coyote.

And the only record, official or unofficial, that I have ever estab-lished came one glorious and lusty day last October when I burned up three and a half boxes of 20-gauge Number 9's without bagging a single woodcock out of the more than seventy-five we flushed that day—not a single one!

No, I'm not an expert outdoorsman by anybody's standards. But to enjoy it, who needs to be? Knowing I can venture into it, however ineptly, is enough to heal my spirit of the wounds inflicted by a too-fast world.

Still, the outdoors means a lot to me.

It is the feeling of wilderness, of unspoiled lands, of streams that I may someday fish, of trails that I have still to find, of mountains seldom climbed—and then sometimes only in my mind.

It is the laughing brooklet that jokes its way through a virgin forest where I shall someday trod, the covert that fairly teems with a grouse that I will unexpectedly discover, and the High Country pasture where the bighorns roam that I will one day see.

It is the quiet meadow where the white-tails feed at twilight, and the hidden marshpond where the bittern groans and where the otters play.

It is becoming blue with cold on a northern deer stand only to become blushingly warm from the excitement generated by a skinny forkhorn running flat-out well beyond shotgun range.

It is toppling into the bunk after a hard day afield, game bag empty, muscles weary, to dream of trophies yet to come, if not to-morrow, perhaps the next, and if not then, the season after.

Hear it? Hear that promise on the wind? Up the hillside, down the valley, through the forest, across the prairie, brushing now your pillow, soothing now your troubled mind.

Hear it?

A Hunter's Morning

The sky was the color of polished butternut and the pond waters were alder-bark grey. A flock of Canada geese should have settled here during the night but they had not come in. Even now, in the icy mists of morning, their haunting cry was missing from the sky.

Instead, the strong south wind of late Indian summer bent the trees. Perhaps the geese, weary from battling the headwind, were resting now on some secluded wilderness lake farther to the north.

So this morning there would be no fat, succulent gander for the table, although by now it mattered little. For the geese had not come down but a giant snowy owl had—just after first light burnished the eastern sky.

The owl had come in slowly and silently over the pond's edge, circled my blind, and fluffed ponderously to a roost on the spar-like remains of an ancient tamarack tree. There it studied me—or so I thought—with sleepy, yellow eyes.

Its attention was disconcerting to say the least but I soon discovered that the owl wasn't savoring me. Several minutes later it shook its great, feathered body and with an instantaneous swoop impaled a struggling red squirrel in its talons.

The squirrel had been my company since along before dawn. Once. I'd even managed to entice it into my blind with a bribe of bread crumbs. And its nervous chattering had signaled the approach of a spikehorn white-tail deer that I would have missed seeing without the squirrel's help.

The drama over, and no geese in sight, it was time to leave the blind. But something held me there—an indistinct feeling that something was about to happen which should not be missed.

Soon, from far up the pond, a playful, splashing sound. It was a pair of otter at play.

As they bubbled within sight of the blind, their curiosity drew them closer. And they pumped their bodies half out of the water to get a better look at the strange, unmoving thing huddled inside a brushpile.

With each heave they voiced their interest with a throaty, blowing sound. I blew back. And they echoed my inept imitation.

My reward for this rudimentary attempt at communication was a water show of comic grace. The otters whirled, swirled, pumped and burped . . . all for my singular benefit. Finally, they tired of the game and swam back up the pond.

In the afterglow of their unexpected performance a lone Canada goose toiled down over the treetops and canted its wings in an approach that would have it alight just fifteen yards from my blind.

By its size and markings it was an old gander, spent and obviously very tired. The wind held him for a long moment and he hovered, wings spread wide and huge webbed feet stretched before him to soften the landing. It was a classic pose and so perfectly executed the scene reminded me of the work of David Maas, the noted wildlife artist.

The proffered shot was an easy one; perhaps the easiest I would ever have. But I made no move to pull my shotgun from its cradle in the gnarled crook of cedar root that served as one side of my blind. So the goose settled down to tuck its head under a wing and soon bobbed peacefully among the wavelets.

I still don't fully understand why I did not take that shot. Perhaps it was just the morning. A hunter's morning. Perhaps being in it had been enough. A goose for the roaster pan could wait for another day. Dinner did not need to be the lone Canada that had flown a thousand miles and more and somehow chose to rest out the day on this particular beaver pond.

As I gathered my gear for the long walk out, I mused over a sudden thought: what would Cleveland Armory or Alice Harrington or the producers of *Say Goodbye* or the *Guns of Autumn* say about this episode?

And then I realized, of course, that those self-styled "Friends of Animals" would say nothing of it, nor could they. For none had ever been a part of a hunter's morning.

I chuckled at the thought. The Canada, startled by the sound, looked about, saw nothing to disturb him further, and nestled back in sleep.

[111]

I lingered for a time, the empty game bag light upon my shoulder, watching the napping gander.

Then, in silent salute, I touched the barrel of my empty shotgun to the visor of my hunting cap, turned, and waded the trail home through autumn-brittle cattail fronds that rustled the pathway closed behind me.

The Regression of Mr. Teal

Mr. Teal ran the blade of his hunting knife around the neck of the bottle, breaking the seal. Then he popped the cork and set the quart of rare Greek brandy in the middle of the picnic table before reaching into the utensil box.

Drawing out a pair of lead crystal goblets from their nest in a velvet-covered layer of plastic foam, he smiled and said, "Time was I could drink a quart of this myself. But I don't anymore. I've learned that moderation is a virtue."

A senior partner in a prosperous law firm that specialized in corporate mergers, Mr. Teal was a gentleman. Polished and sophisticated, many said his bearing reminded them of John Connally, the former governor of Texas, for Mr. Teal had silver hair, spoke in a resonant, perfectly modulated voice, and was always impeccably dressed and groomed, even while tent camping at his favorite lakeside campsite deep in the Northwoods.

Perhaps that's why those of us who occasionally hunted with him—a generally disheveled lot, inclined to slothful habits and attire when afield—always addressed him as *Mister* Teal. Somehow, as much as we liked him, we could never bring ourselves to call him by his first name, which was Fenton, nor by devising an appropriate nickname for him.

Mr. Teal seemed to accept the formality, although I noticed that whenever we introduced him to one of our unkempt friends he was quick to acknowledge with the words, "Yes, *Teal* . . . just like the duck."

Over the years, Mr. Teal had acquired two passions: a taste of 100-proof brandy and an addiction to woodcock hunting. He indulged them both on these crisp late September weekends when the migratory flocks from Canada would stop over to rest on the leeward slopes of the aspen-covered hills in the sunlit lowlands surrounding the lake.

[113]

Most of those who hunted here, however, considered woodcock hunting akin to coot hunting. They classified both birds as edible only under survival conditions. This weekend, with the opening of ruffed grouse season still two weeks away, and trout season over, Mr. Teal and I had the campground to ourselves.

"Help yourself," Mr. Teal motioned toward the bottle.

Carefully, I poured the liquid down the side of the glass until the goblet was one-third full. Then I held it toward the glow of the setting sun. Its color was that of buckwheat honey, but with a slight purple cast.

"I see you have a feeling for fine brandy," Mr. Teal said. "To truly enjoy it one must savor it with the eyes before savoring it with the palate."

"It's as you taught me, Mr. Teal," I said, enjoying the first sip. He seemed pleased by the remark.

"Acquiring a taste for fine brandy is like developing a lust for woodcock hunting," he explained. "Once learned, both habits force overindulgence which one must learn to temper."

I sipped the brandy which was somewhat oily and aroused the delicate tissues inside my mouth. To cool my tongue I expelled air with a quiet *woosh*.

"Ah, yes," said Mr. Teal, "fine brandy has fire."

He swirled his glass and looked across the lake into the glow of the rising moon. "There's frost in the air tonight. A good omen. This is the kind of weather that will tempt the flight birds to settle in. We should have fair shooting in the morning."

As we talked the level of the liquid in the bottle steadily diminished.

"Yes, my boy," said Mr. Teal, mellow now, and looser, "time was when I not only managed to drink a quart of brandy in a single evening's sitting, but also arise at dawn to shoot any legal game that walked, hopped, flew, ran or slithered. I thought the whole idea of hunting was to put as much meat in my gamebag as the law would allow . . . sometimes more than the law would allow."

He sloshed another measure of brandy into his goblet before continuing. "Then, much later, I decided it didn't make sense to shoot *everything* so I took up trophy hunting. I've a roomful of heads from the corners of the world. But that practice soon revealed itself for what it was, a random competition with a list of unkown names in the record books. And one day it struck me that trophy shooting didn't make any more sense than meat hunting. That's when I took up woodcock. I was about fifty. And, if I recall, I quit overindulging in brandy about the same time."

He reached for the bottle and poured another. "Now, I'm convinced that there is no finer pleasure on earth than a leisurely hunt for woodcock during these migratory flights. You seldom meet another hunter in the coverts. The birds are prolific enough so that you can pick your shot and leave the probables go by. And a half-dozen woodcock breasts is enough for anyone. Baked in wine they are a gourmet's delight."

I nodded in agreement and placed my empty glass on the table.

"My goodness," said Mr. Teal. "We've killed the quart."

Then he smiled and dropped the empty bottle into the trash container. "Well," he said tentatively, "I suppose it's only human nature to occasionally regress."

Saturday morning dawned clear and brisk. We waited for the autumn sun to burn the wetness off the undergrowth and left the tent to hunt in the perfection of a colorful September day.

On a hillside not twenty yards from the campsite, Mr. Teal's Irish setter, Oliver, flushed the first bird of the day. Mr. Teal took it, an easy crossing shot.

I walked my Brittany, Doc, away from Mr. Teal to cover an adjacent ridgeline. There was no question the flight was in, for the hillsides were alive with resting woodcock which helicoptered upward at nearly every step.

An hour later, Doc had pointed more than two dozen birds and I had tucked six into the gamepocket of my jacket. Recalling Mr. Teal's words, "a half-dozen is enough for anyone," I returned to the campsite.

Mr. Teal was not there so I cleaned my birds and put them in the cooler. Then I set about preparing breakfast—sourdough pancakes, Canadian bacon topped with cheddar cheese, and two eggs each, sunnyside up.

Every few minutes I heard echoes of shotguns reverberate among the hills. Obviously Mr. Teal and I were not the only hunters who considered woodcock hunting pleasurable.

About noon, Mr. Teal walked up the graveled path, Oliver panting beside him, and hung his coat on the stub of a tree near the picnic table.

"Your breakfast is cold, Mr. Teal. How did the hunting go?"

"My boy," he said, "this is the most fantastic shooting of my life. I stopped counting flushes at seventy-five or so. I . . . ah . . . may have overdone it."

He reached for his hunting coat and began to pull out birds. " . . . fifteen . . . ah . . . sixteen . . . seventeen," he counted. "What's the limit anyway?"

"Fifteen."

"How many did you take, my boy?" he asked, the color rising in his cheeks."

"A half-dozen is enough for anyone," I reminded him.

"Well now," Mr. Teal said in his resonant, perfectly modulated voice, "I suppose it's only human nature to occasionally regress."

Oliver yawned, stretched, and crawled under the table where he flopped down in the warm sand to curl up in sleep.

Laurel Hill

*T*here is a place that I return to often in my mind . . . a place called Laurel Hill.

I call it that because the mountain laurels, when I knew it, grew there farther north than the botanists said they had the ability to grow.

The laurels, as I remember them, clung to the rounded slopes of a glacial esker deep within a hidden valley.

Once, on a misty October morning, I walked the perimeter of Laurel Hill and grouse exploded like a salvo of grey thunderballs.

At least I *think* that's how it was, because today I'm not sure that there ever was a Laurel Hill, nor am I certain that the grouse which lived upon it were truly as prolific as I remember them.

Were there actually *coveys* of grouse, as I now recall? Or was there only a brace of grouse which in its thunderous leaving compelled me to think that the misty hillside abounded in them? Were there any grouse at all? Perhaps I merely heard the rustle of brittle autumn leaves accosted by a sudden gust of southbound wind and *thought* the birds were there. The shapes I saw leaving might have been nothing more than a flock of Canada jays.

Whatever the circumstances, I vividly recall that misty autumn morning when I first walked Laurel Hill.

There, beyond the highway bridge, around the first bend in the river, and then over the scrub oak ridgeline to that unexpected valley—a slash of green tucked low among the fiery autumn highlands . . . and in the valley the quarter-mile elongated rising of Laurel Hill, its slopes fairly teeming with grouse.

Fortune must have guided me that day, for I wasn't seriously hunting . . . I was merely meandering the bottomland along the river, caught up in the exhilaration of being afield on a magnificent October morning.

It had been a dry year and I reasoned that any grouse remaining in this country would be near water. But I didn't really expect to flush a grouse nor did I envision that I would find them in such profusion as I now think they were on Laurel Hill.

The first grouse burst into my autumn-induced heedlessness like the ring of an alarm clock on the second morning of deer season—I heard it but I could not respond.

And then came another bird . . . and another. Grouse exploded everywhere. At first, I thought I'd stumbled into a covey of quail. But the birds were larger, their flight more erratic. And it was seconds before I knew that the sounds around me were caused by the King of the Uplands, the elusive ruffed grouse.

Slowly. S-l-o-w-l-y. Ever so slowly. I mounted my 20-gauge over-and-under and pulled the front trigger, then the rear trigger. And in so doing I made the upland gunner's number-one mistake: I shot at the flock and not at *a* bird.

They boomed away unscathed. At least a dozen of them . . . or so it seemed.

Then, a slight rise of Laurel Hill later, another flock burst forth. Again, startled, I emptied the gun only to miss twice more.

By now the birdy activity at Laurel Hill had jogged me into becoming extremely cautious. Gingerly, at each step, I probed the forest floor with the toe of my boot and finding no desiccated twig to crackle under my weight I would gently lower my heel.

So when the next flock went up I was alert and ready. Calmly, I picked a bird, downed it, then selectively I sighted on another which also dropped earthward and momentarily fluttered at the base of a tree. A double on grouse! My first!

Doc, my hyperactive Brittany, who up to now had been as lethargic as I about hunting and had contented himself with nuzzling for field mice under the fallen leaves, saw the two birds drop and dashed from one to the other on the retrieve. He was so excited that he didn't know which bird to claim first.

Finally, when he had calmed himself enough to recognize that he had work to do, he fetched each bird, in turn, to my side.

When I examined these unexpected creatures, I found to my surprise that both were "chocolate" grouse. Their tails were the deep, rich brown of a Hershey candy bar. Not russet, not bronzed silver, but chocolate brown. The rarest variation of this dichromatic species.

I *know* that happened on Laurel Hill. I have the chocolate fans displayed, today, in my living room. They are stapled to bamboo wands and delicately arranged in the Japanese tradition to flare from the mouth of a stoneware butter churn that is at least a century old.

And every day, when I look at them, I yearn to return to Laurel Hill.

But no matter how hard I try, I've never again been fortunate enough to find it.

Each October, I go to the bridge, follow the winding river, walk the scrub oak ridgeline, and meander the bottomland. But in a half-dozen seasons of searching, I've yet to rediscover that tiny valley, still green in autumn, where the chocolate grouse abound on a place that I call Laurel Hill.

Perhaps I was so excited that day that I simply presumed there was a valley lined in unseasonable greenery. It might have been nothing more than a lowland pine plantation.

And the hill might not have been truly a hill, but merely a slight upwelling of the land among the seeded pines.

And the unusual trees I saw—the mountain laurel—might not have been an orchard but a single tree that could have been planted by a homesteader many years ago and which has survived long after the farmstead was abandoned and planted over with the pine.

Perhaps Laurel Hill never was. Perhaps, I sometimes think, I only imagined it.

And then I touch the chocolate-colored fans that tassle now from the antique butter churn.

There is a Laurel Hill . . . I'm sure of it. And I'll search for it again one misty and mysterious morning this October.

[119]

An Element of Risk

When our neighbor's college-age daughter came home on semester break and announced that she had signed up for sky-diving lessons, her mother was horrified. "Why kids nowadays want to go out and kill themselves is beyond me," Mom complained.

Why indeed, I thought. For the fastest growing outdoor sports today—hang gliding, sky diving, rock climbing, wilderness back-packing, Nordic skiing, whitewater canoeing and scuba diving—are drawing followers like a new lettuce patch draws cottontail. Is it a passing phenomenon? Or is it that these risk sports offer something that is missing from the routine life we've sought to create for ourselves? The closer we come to our supposed ideal of cradle-to-grave security, it appears, the more we seem to wish to engage in leisure activities that offer a flavor of danger and an element of risk.

There is, of course, ample evidence in history to show that man is a creature who thrives only when he is free to risk. And that proclivity may separate him from lesser creatures. Perhaps without it man would not be man but would be, instead, just another social animal.

Consider, for example, those of us who risk free diving in scuba gear to depths that seasoned hard-hat divers would not have dared only a few years ago. Why do we do it?

We're testing ourselves! No doubt about it. We want to discover our limits. We like that charged-up feeling that comes from preparing to risk and the exuberance that overcomes us when we succeed. And to experience that momentary euphoria, we readily accept the possibility of failure and also its consequences.

When Janet Guthrie, the first woman to compete in the Indianapolis 500 was asked why she worked so long and so hard to qualify for an event that might result in her injury or death, she replied: "There is very little in our advanced civilization that requires you to extend yourself to the limits, physically, mentally and emotionally. For me, Indianapolis is where it's at."

In the earlier days of our country, we did not need to seek risk. Living itself was a tenuous proposition. There were hazards in merely stepping out the back door.

Later, the Depression of the 1930's, World War II in the 1940's, Korea in the 1950's, and Vietnam in the 1960's added the specter of danger to our lives, the male lives, at least.

Even today, in primitive societies, individuals discover early in life how far they can extend themselves—how much they can take—during manhood rituals and puberty rites.

But in our society we have so civilized the process of risk taking that it is only acceptable to expose ourselves to peril after we reach the age of majority and then, only after working hours. So on weekends we soar out of the sun under a flimsy triangular patch of nylon cloth, or kayak a Class V whitewater rapids. Then, on Monday morning, exhausted, scratched and bruised, we tell co-workers how great we feel. And we do!

The more sedentary among us have outlets, too: Hunting, fishing, backcountry camping, rifle shooting, trap and skeet, all afford us the chance to fail in a way that will neither be harmful to us nor upset society's long-standing mores. Engaging in them is enough to satisfy our innate desire for competition. Pursuing them keeps us out of mischief during idle hours. And they are ideal, too, for the risk training of our youth.

Have you ever met, for example, a juvenile delinquent who has spent time afield with a veteran at his side to show the way? I've not.

Exposing a youngster to the risk of wading to a rising trout on a quiet midsummer stream, then guiding him progressively to fish swifter waters, teaches him to accept a challenge, coaches him in the benefits of caution, and trains him to recognize and assess risk. That lesson learned, the youngster need not look elsewhere for kicks or highs.

Consider the consequences of banning hunting or regulating the use of sporting arms so that few would have access to them. Opportunities for risk training would be lost. And without that training there's a good chance that youth will seek risk elsewhere, perhaps in more destructive ways.

Risk training always pays off. No question of it. The youngster who has learned to risk knows his limitations. He knows what he can do and, more important, he knows what he cannot do.

And later, most who have received early risk training generally demonstrate its value. They seem to be equipped to extrapolate earlier experiences into other risky situations: A critical diagnosis in a hospital surgery, a line of inquiry in a research laboratory, a command decision on a battlefield, a judgment in a corporate boardroom, or an instantaneous response to a flashing red light on the control panel of a space shuttle.

In contrast, think of those who have never been exposed to risk training. They have never been taught to fail, therefore they always will.

The circumstances of youngsters unfortunate enough to have been born in a ghetto come quickly to mind. They face nearly insurmountable odds from the moment of birth. Here, risk training can show that they can sometimes win. A small success or two could supply the incentive to win more, and win bigger, canceling the idea that in their environment anything one tries is doomed to failure.

Lack of risk training, too, might be what accounts for the sporadic achievements of the women's movement. Never having been taught to risk, it equates being assertive with being aggressive. As a result, a momentary loss is considered a major defeat. And paranoid-like, the movement howls foul whenever it doesn't get its way.

Perhaps the upsurge in girls' competitive team sports in elementary and high schools will eventually teach women that to risk means to accept the possibility of failure.

All of us need an element of risk in our lives. Indeed, we have a *right* to it.

And those who advocate otherwise know, I think, that if they can deny the opportunity to risk they will also restrict our capability to make reasoned choices. Thus removing the most effective means we have to resist their domination.

On the strength of that thought, I think I'll go sky-diving tomorrow.

Won't you join me?

Someday

*T*oday, the thing that wasn't supposed to happen did: Someday has come.

It came on me unawares out of the enervation of this sub-zero Saturday which is too blustery for cross-country skiing, ice fishing or even snowshoe hare hunting. Football season, too, is past and there's nothing else of merit on TV. And, miraculously, my job jar is empty—somehow all my household chores have been completed.

Now, after a dozen years of hoarding spent shotgun shells on the premise that someday I'd get around to reloading them and thereby save a bundle of money in my shooting and hunting activities, I've got the spare time to fill a few seasons' worth with new shot and powder.

But I've put aside several other tasks for Someday, too: refinishing the canoe; repairing battered duck decoys; patching leaking waders, replacing squished guides and flattened ferrules on a half-dozen fishing rods, and reblueing the receiver and barrels of my favorite over-and-under.

Which should I do first, now that Someday has come? That question is my dilemma . . . You know how it is.

Then I recall that my friend Big Ed once referred to the tasks we save up for Someday as "to-its." (Derived, I suppose, from the statement, "Someday I'll get around to it.")

"To-its," said Big Ed, "serve as reminders that you'll always have something requiring your special talents to put right. That's their only value. If you run out of them well . . . there's no reason for you to stick around."

"How's that?" I remember asking.

"Show me a person," Big Ed replied, "who has accumulated a large number of to-its and I'll show you a person who will remain spry and hardy well past the biblical fourscore and ten. To-its give you something to look forward to in life."

So today, with the howling of the blizzard muted by the storm windows and with the cherry-wood logs crackling on the hearth, inviting me to enjoy their warmth, I find Big Ed's reasoning easy to accept. I really don't want to get around to anything, although I realize that Someday has finally come.

Still, that sort of thinking makes me feel uneasy. Laziness is the tool of the Devil and I hesitate to succumb.

Instead, I rationalize. Those shotgun hulls won't deteriorate with age, I can reload them another time.

And I don't need any extra serviceable fishing rods; when each of the old was broken I immediately replaced it with another made of better, modern materials.

Neither is the leak in my waders something that needs prompt attention—it's only a pinhole and the cold water it allows to trickle down my left leg forces me to be a more active angler.

Now that I think about it, too, the finish on the canoe and the blueing on the shotgun aren't in such a state that they can't last another season.

And it's been my experience (I tell myself) that battered decoys attract more waterfowl then do perfect blocks highlighted in sun-glistening new paint.

Yet Someday has come and it seems a waste not to use it to advantage, for something productive. So I run a mental finger down my list of to-its and, one by one, I isolate several, the disposition of which will assuage my do-something conscience on this perfect take-a-nap day.

I've been meaning, I decide, to try out that Christmas-gift cornpopper using some of Danny Kroll's special hybrid popping corn.

And if I'm to do that, what better time to taste-test that new batch of wild grape wine? It's been fermenting in a stoneware crock since late September.

Then, too, munching buttered popcorn before a cheery fire while sipping the sweetness of my Northwoods nectar lends itself to reading. Haven't I been meaning to get around to immersing myself in George Bird Evans' recently published book *Recollections of a Shooting Guest*?

I dribble the golden kernels into the wire basket and stoke the coals to promote an even popping. "Sandberg," I chuckle to myself in satisfaction, "you've brought it off! You've truly done it, boy! In a single stroke of genius you've managed to eliminate three to-its and still you've plenty of them remaining to take care of another Someday, should it ever come again."

Among the Stars

Once, on a crisp and clear September night, when the moon hung pumpkin-orange in a cavernous sky of vitreous purple, we sat around our campfire at Camp One Rapids Pool and saw curious orbs of intense white light gambol in the space between the stars.

More than a dozen flitted about, sometimes resting in circular array, often creating a pattern which suggested that the angels might be playing a heavenly game of duck-duck-goose . . . in three dimensions.

Occasionally, one light would elect, for some inexplicable reason, to helicopter several thousand feet straight up from the others. Then it would hover there for a time before swiftly descending to its former place in the strange arrangement.

So we sat, in that haunting September twilight, gazing outward from the campfire's cheery glow, visually linking ourselves into a part of the universe that was light years beyond our own.

"Weather balloons?" Carol ventured.

"No," I disagreed, "they're too high and too mobile . . . jet-stream winds aren't that erratic."

"Space probes," one of the twins said, "waiting for the Mother Ship."

"Unlikely," I replied. "Technology isn't that far along."

"They could be Russian," the other twin suggested.

As the chill of the autumn night drew us closer to the fire, conversation faltered and each of us retreated inward to be secure in more familiar thoughts.

The warmth of the fire, the long miles I'd trudged that day searching for a migratory flight of woodcock, the hearty supper preceded by several applications of my favorite internal liniment, all quietly

[126]

combined to lull my senses. In a drowsy state of semi-being I watched the hypnotic pattern of the lights and speculated about their origins.

Soon, I felt my mind, which had somehow become detached from my body, being drawn upward to join the shining spheres that flitted now among the stars.

As I floated weightlessly, the blaze of the roaring after-supper campfire far below quickly diminished to a ruddy glow, then disappeared in blackness.

Strangely, I still felt whole, although my body seemed to have remained by the fire below. Curiously, too, my senses continued to operate much as before, but more slowly, and with greater perceptiveness. Indeed, I tingled. It was a pleasant feeling.

Soon the earth itself, a luminous blue disc streaked with white cloud and splashes of tie-dyed greens and browns, was no larger than a vinyl beach ball. Then it, too, was lost in darkness.

Drifting now in soft black velvet, I heard a thought being imposed into my mind. It was not my own:

"You come from a Twenty-third Psalm place. There is no other like it. It is filled with wondrous things. Great deeds will soon be accomplished there. You will have a part in them."

Then came another thought, this time in verse:

"Every single blade of grass,
and every flake of snow,
is just a wee bit different,
there's no two alike, you know."

In succession, other thoughts were thrust at me, imprinting themselves forever on my mind. They came rapidly, from every direction, and my mind fairly reeled from their impact.

Then a sudden realization: the thoughts were moving in precisely the same pattern as had the unusual lights we'd watched from far below.

I saw clearly, too, that many of the thoughts had been implanted long ago, and since forgotten. The first, in fact, was that of Lee Dreyfus, the articulate Governor of the State of Wisconsin. I'd been inspired by his speeches many times.

And the second—that delightful verse—was the thought of Deb Moir, a teenager from Edmonton, Alberta, Canada. I'd read it in an Ann Landers column.

I recognized, too, the origins of several other thoughts. But many came that I had no recollection of ever having heard. All, however, were good thoughts, and generally profound.

How had my mind escaped my body to travel starward? Why? Were the lights we'd seen simply thoughts that had somehow materialized? Did they now have the power to attract lesser thoughts to them, thereby to polish and improve, to teach by example?

The idea, I decide, is not as far-fetched as it first appears. Everyone has had such unusual experiences. The phenomenon is universal.

For I recall reading, in one of Isaac Asimov's brilliant books, that all of the atoms of our bodies, except hydrogen, were once at the core of stars that exploded sometime during the 20-billion-year history of our universe.

So I conclude that I am kin to everyone and everything. A piece of me is first cousin to a piece of you. We share the same primal energy with Lee Dreyfus, Deb Moir, the earth, the stars and, yes, even the energy of our thoughts is shared.

"Likes attract" is by now, too, a proven and familiar physical law. Therefore wouldn't thoughts tend to be drawn together in some special place? Where better for them to gather than in the space between the stars?

And since thoughts have primal energy, wouldn't they radiate light? Wouldn't they *be* lights?

With that, I felt myself descending earthward as rapidly as I'd been drawn away before.

First the earth hove into view, then I saw the campfire's ruddy glow, and then I was seated by the flames, wide awake, refreshed.

"Did you see that?" Carol was saying.

"What?"

"Another light just joined the others. Then suddenly it fell away . . . like a falling star. I thought it would drop right into the fire . . . but it burned out just above the treetops."

One of the twins, stifling a yawn, looked up and said brightly, "I've got it! The lights are UFO's."

"Yes," I agreed. "they're all of that . . . and more."

The Bend in the River

There was no roadside mailbox, the driveway hadn't been used in months, and the tiny, century-old farmhouse hadn't been treated to fresh paint in years. But the old man taking the noonday sun on its porch looked unusually cheerful, so I waved casually to him from the unpaved township road as I walked by.

"Come, sit a spell," the old man beckoned.

Weary from an unproductive morning of chasing grouse across the parched ridgelines of the Thunder River backcountry, I climbed the porch to gratefully accept a dipper of cold well water.

"Thanks," I said, smiling. "How do they make it so good and sell it so cheap?"

"Young man," he admonished me, "*they* didn't make it. He did."

"Of course," I stammered. "No offense . . . just trying to make conversation . . . This water sure tastes sweet."

He fidgeted for a moment in his wheel chair and rearranged himself by clasping both hands under a knee and tugging each leg, in turn, to a more comfortable position. "How was the hunting?"

"Three flushed; three missed," I grimaced.

"Used to be that way with me," he laughed, "up until I fell out of the hay mow a few years back. Ruffed grouse are elusive creatures.

"When the weather is nice," he continued, "and when I can get one of the neighbor boys to haul me and this damned chair into the woods, I still manage some squirrel hunting. But I really miss the grouse."

"I know what you mean," I said, gulping down another dipperful of the throat-soothing water.

Soon this pleasant gentleman—there is no other way to describe him, for he was indeed that—had me detailing how and where I'd flushed each bird that morning. His eyes sparkled as I recounted, with only minor embellishments, how the first had taken a screech-

ing ninety-degree turn around a spruce tree the moment I shot. And
he nodded vigorously, sparse strands of silver-white hair dancing
across his forehead, when I told him how another had flushed directly into my face.

"They'll do that to you," he chuckled as he began to reminisce.

He told me about his days as a market hunter when he and his
partner had piled grouse and ducks "waist-high to a Swede lumberjack" at North Country railheads for shipment to Chicago markets.

"At the time," he recalled, "fifteen cents a bird was pretty good
pay. And we were naive enough to believe that the birds would
never run out."

He related, too, how he'd once taken three white-tail bucks within
ten minutes of each other with successive, single shots from his
.44-40 Winchester.

"Never bought more than five bullets a season," he chortled. "Never needed more."

Then he told me about brook trout fishing and sawmilling and trapping and whiskey making and the attributes of having to use an outdoor toilet when it was twenty below zero. "You don't linger while responding to nature's call," he related. "Not when the alternative is frostbite on a cherished body part."

Then suddenly, breaking his own reverie, he said: "Tell you what, young man . . . If you promise to bring me a bird for my Sunday supper, I'll show you how to get to the best grousing place in this country. It was my favorite. I've never told anyone about it before."

Eagerly I agreed, envisioning a place so abundant in fat, overmature, unmolested grouse that I'd need a Duluth pack to tote them out in a single trip.

He pulled the stub of a pencil from his pocket, rummaged through a pile of magazines on the wicker sidetable near his chair, and began to sketch rapidly on an old envelope he'd found there. "First," he said,"you walk through the back pasture and down the lane to the bend in the river . . ."

Late that afternoon, when I'd had enough of tromping through this unseasonably warm Indian summer day, I returned to the lane and trudged toward the farmhouse. The hot orange sun was touching the treetops in the west and the moon, cold white-gold in a cloudless sky, had already risen.

"You don't appear to be overburdened," the old man bristled as I neared the porch.

"No," I replied. "I didn't put up a bird."

"I expected as much," he said sadly. "Grouse move out when the woods grow up. No food. No cover. Old growth doesn't offer them much reason to stay around. But I had to know . . . you understand."

"I found the place where you shot those deer," I said brightly. "Your chair is still there . . . just where you'd said it would be. And there are fresh droppings on the runways."

"You don't say?" He seemed cheered by the news.

"Yes. And I spotted a good place to ambush ducks just downstream of the river bend. The water should still be open there when the bluebills come down from Canada in November."

"But no grouse," he repeated.

"No grouse," I acknowledged.

[131]

We talked for a time about the woods he still loved so dearly after all these years. And I understood him better.

By now the moon was high and glaringly white over the fields. I stretched, picked up my shotgun and jumped off the porch. "It's late. Time to go. And my wife's a bear when I miss supper."

"Thanks for stopping by," he said. "Come back anytime. And if you want to build a duck blind on the river, just go ahead. Bluebill ain't as tasty as grouse but any wild game will be a treat."

Several weeks later, when I returned to hunt the late bluebill season, the house was locked and the snow was windrowed across the porch, undisturbed. I knocked several times and called: "Anybody home?" But no one answered.

And that's when I realized, with a sudden futility, *I never knew his name.*

Building a Dream

I like to read about places I shall never see and trophies I shall never claim, be they $100 away on the Mississippi River or $10,000 away in Kenya.

I know, for example, that I will never afford an elephant hunt in Africa. And the possibilities of taking a charter fishing trip on Lake Michigan, closer to home, are equally at variance with the thickness of my wallet.

But there's a chance that someday I might do both, for among the inalienable rights of man is the right to dream of things that have no right to happen but sometimes will.

Once, in that strange and velvet sleep typical of early morning, I dreamed of how I would one day buy a parcel of land "Up North" and build upon it the most exquisite of log cabins.

Our cabin would have a great fieldstone fireplace along one wall and an even greater screened veranda along the northwest side so I could sit, on a summer evening, and watch the beauty of the setting sun.

And it would be entirely decorated in a mode that can best be described as "Sportsman's Whimsy."

The plaque displaying the perfect rack from the six-point white-tail I took many years ago—my first—would be above the fireplace mantel. The mantel, of course, would be a hand-hewn beam from an old barn that had been built in the same year the Territorial Papers were signed. And splendidly arrayed upon it would be all my old and valued duck decoys.

There would be a place, too, for hanging the mount of the sixteen-inch perch I took one misty and glorious September morning from Chalk Hill flowage on the Menominee River. And next to that would hang an even greater fish—a sixteen-pound brown trout from Lake Michigan.

Then, near this display of trophies—the meager bag from a lifetime of hunting and fishing in the Northwoods, but highly valued nonetheless—I would build a bookcase.

The bookcase would be enormous, covering an entire paneled wall, for it would need to hold the magazines and books that I will dream upon once I get tired of watching the red squirrels and chipmunks which dominate my new-bought land.

Sometimes I think about this and I can actually picture myself sitting before that fire, lolled out in an antique genuine-leather couch, a brandy old-fashioned in one hand, and the other ruffling the neck of my faithful grouse dog, Doc, a Brittany who has a nose for birds that won't quit—robins, crows, sparrows, even grackles, but never a grouse nor a woodcock.

I dream about this picturesque setting at dawn . . . then I wake up.

How can we ever afford a place in the woods? The milk bill is due, so is the mortgage payment . . . and the oil bill . . . and the electric bill.

The girls start college next year, too. Where will I get the thousands of dollars for that?

And the car is dripping oil on the driveway . . . and . . . and . . . and.

Bills. Bills. Bills.

You know how it is.

To make matters worse, my wife confronts me with the question: "Why can't we go out to eat tonight?"

And she goes on: "The girls at work always talk about the good food at Gene's Supper Club. Why don't we go there?"

Lamely, I rationalize about inflationary processes and lecture her about how the Federal Reserve System sets interest rates and therefore dictates our financial fortune which, at the moment, I assure her, is extremely bleak.

But she works keeping books for a multi-national corporation and doesn't buy a word of that.

So I say, quite bluntly. "We can't afford it."

"Can't afford it!" she replies. "You bought that new grouse hunting book for $12.95. If we can afford that, surely we can afford to go out for a cheap dinner." (Emphasis, of course, on "cheap.")

How can I explain that the grouse hunting book is the only thing between me, the horror of contemplating inflation, and the fear of catching one of those severe neuroses which afflict modern, urban man?

Upon the paragraphs of that book I've built the dreams which sustain me Monday through Friday, between weekend outings. There's no question of it, to me at least, that the $12.95 spent to quell the disturbances within me is worth several times the price.

For dreams, I've learned, are more important than eating in these agitating times—there are so few chances to indulge in the former than in the latter.

Then, too, no matter how hard one tries, it is difficult to catch a dream.

The reason is simple: after you've caught it, the dream is no longer there. It has become reality. The illusion is no more.

So it's wise to nourish future dreams by investing extra money now and then in magazines and books whose contents tend to feed your fantasies.

And that determination has perpetuated within me, over a period of years, the dream of getting away from it all to the Northwoods.

So one day I announced: "We're going to sell this house and head for the North Country. If we don't go now we never shall.

"We can look for some acreage on a lake or on a good trout stream and build a cabin precisely to our needs. We'll have everything we've always wanted."

"Except," some pessimistic listener said, "a full stomach. How do you propose to eat?"

The question was unanswerable, so we're still here, living from paycheck to paycheck, eating regularly, paying outrageous taxes, being miserable.

But we're still building a dream—of living in a wild forest laced with flowing crystal waters where pileated woodpeckers still choose to roam. And someday, if we work hard enough, we might actually do it.

With that thought, I riffle through a copy of a nationally circulated outdoor magazine and pause to read an interesting article about catching monster rainbow trout in Patagonia, on the southern tip of South America.

But soon I close the page, realizing full well that I shall never travel there.

Still, I might make it next season to that fish-filled North Country lake Old Joe Hallen once told me about. "It's secluded," he said, "seldom fished, and hauntingly beautiful."

Even if I am unable to arrange the trip—reaching it will require a canoe, another item I don't have the money to buy—I won't be too concerned. For I've already done the next best thing to being there: I've built a dream.

And tomorrow I shall build another.

Tulip and The McGregor

*I*n the North Country, where names such as Mike and Joe and Bill are common, any man unfortunate enough to have been christened Shellburne Flowers was certain to acquire a nickname early in life. Since Shellburne's surname was what it was and also because he was oversized and angular, with that special gentleness big men often have, naturally we'd called him "Tulip"—from early on.

In contrast, Tulip's frequent companion was a wiry and fiery Scotsman whom everyone called The McGregor. No one called him Mr. McGregor, or simply McGregor, or by his first name which was Sam. He was always called *The* McGregor, as if there would never be another like him.

Tulip and The McGregor were the finest woodsmen in the county and they were particularly addicted to white-tail deer hunting. One or the other invariably won the annual Big Buck contest sponsored by Pete Peterson's Sporting Goods store. And someone once said he'd seen them walking by a department store window during the Christmas shopping season when a stuffed reindeer leaped out of the display and dashed down the street, so frightened was it of their considerable reputations.

The story was almost believable, since everyone knew the pair preferred to live off the land rather than succumb to the security of that peculiar affliction of civilized man called a steady job. "Turtles don't work," The McGregor was fond of saying, "and they generally live to be well past a hundred."

Not that Tulip and The McGregor were either lazy or slovenly; they were not. Their equipment was always in good repair and ready for instantaneous use. They were students of their chosen vocation, too, always willing to try any new technique or gadget that promised to

[137]

give them an edge on their quarry of the moment. They were the first in the county, for example, to use compund bows, graphite flyrods, chart-recording depth sounders, and no-wax cross country skis.

Once, sometime during a rather uneventful bowhunting season, The McGregor learned of a new product guaranteed to change their luck which, until that time, had been miserable.

"The deer are staying away from all their usual spots," Tulip complained. "Maybe you should take a bath, McGregor." (Tulip was the only person who could call McGregor simply McGregor, perhaps because he didn't wish to acknowledge his friend as someone special.)

"You don't smell much like your name yourself," replied The McGregor squinting at Tulip with hard, steely black eyes. "And you know darn well that soap and other sweet-smelling stuff will actually drive the deer away. Anyway, I think I've got our no-deer problem solved."

"Oh?" said Tulip.

"Yup. My good friend Maynard Mickelson from Black River Falls sent me a sample of a new buck lure he calls *Rut*. Maynard says the stuff is so powerful the government made him print a caution on the label. Here, take a look." He handed Tulip a glass medicine bottle, the kind that has a built-in dropper for a stopper.

Tulip held the bottle to the light and read aloud: *Warning. This lure may be dangerous to put on your clothing when deer, elk or moose are in their rutting season. Please read instructions inside of box.*

"If it's so powerful," said Tulip, "why aren't all the bow hunters using it?"

"Maynard makes it out of liquids taken from live doe during their estrous period. He has a limited number of captive deer so he can't produce more than a small amount of scent annually. And most of that he gives to his best friends."

"Sounds reasonable," agreed Tulip.

"It is," The McGregor assured him. "Can you think of a better way to entice a horny buck than with the odor of a potential lover in heat? It should work much better than those apple scents we've tried, or those dried leg glands we've ground up and dispersed in mineral oil."

Tulip nodded. "So all we need to do is squirt some *Rut* around our tree stands and the bucks will come in from miles around."

"Not quite," said The McGregor. "It isn't as easy as that. Maynard says white-tails have learned to stay clear of tree stands when they detect man-scent nearby."

"Then what good is the stuff?"

"Well . . . Maynard's thought of that, too. First you soak a ball of cotton in *Rut* and tie it to a bush near your stand. That will draw them in. Then you fake them out by masking your human odor with skunk essence."

"Skunk essence?"

"That's what Maynard recommends."

"Sounds like a smelly proposition to me," Tulip responded dourly.

"Our luck has been bad all season," The McGregor reminded him. "What have we got to lose? Let's give Maynard's method a try."

Early the next morning, in the half-light of an overcast dawn, Tulip and The McGregor cautiously approached a deeply rutted white-tail runway inside the edge of a vast cedar swamp that bordered some upland alfalfa fields. Each of them had killed deer here in past seasons by sitting in the spreading branches of a pair of sprawling oak trees that guarded each leg of a "Y" in the trail. The trees grew within talking range of the hunters and were ideal for ambushing morning deer. The idea was to intercept the animals as they meandered in from their nightly feast in the uplands, stuffed and content.

Following Maynard's printed instruction sheet, they saturated cotton balls with *Rut* and hung them in the open areas near their three stands. Then they sprinkled skunk essence in the tracks they'd walked and climed to their seats in the oaks.

About halfway to his perch, Tulip slipped on the wet bark and tumbled heavily to the ground.

"Oh, no!" The McGregor heard Tulip moan.

"Are you hurt?"

"No, it's worse than that," Tulip gasped, trying to recapture the wind that had been partially knocked out of his lungs by the fall.

"Worse. Did you break your bow?"

"The scent bottles are smashed . . . both of them. They were in my hip pocket. My clothes are soaked with the stuff. It's horrible."

The McGregor clambered down from his tree and rushed to help. Sniffing, he stopped twenty yards short of where Tulip lay at the base of the oak. "My God!" he said. "I can smell you from here! Take off your clothes and go wash in the creek. Then I'll drive you home. You can ride in the back of the pick-up."

"It's too cold to undress."

"Well," said The McGregor, "you're not going to stink up my vehicle. You either get rid of those clothes or you walk home; take your choice."

Slowly, Tulip undressed, his teeth chattering.

"Those, too," said The McGregor, pointing to Tulip's long-johns.

"No, not the underwear," Tulip shook his head firmly. "I'm not going to ride into town stark naked in the back of a pick-up truck."

"There's a blanket in the cab. You can wrap it around yourself."

Then, just as Tulip had pulled the long-johns to his ankles, a huge white-tail buck, drawn perhaps by the vile mixture of scents that now hung sickeningly around the area, snorted and crashed from the screening brush that hid the trail. And the buck, spotting Tulip struggling to pull his feet from the clinging underwear, stopped abruptly to study the scene in near-sighted bewilderment. It sniffed twice, to satisfy its confused senses that the strange creature it smelled was indeed a potential lover who somehow had gotten sprayed by a skunk, then it snorted loudly, pawed the earth, and lowered its head to charge.

"The damn thing thinks you're a doe," The McGregor chortled from the safety of twenty yards. "Don't turn your back on him or he'll nail you for sure."

"Shoot him, McGregor!" Tulip cried. "Don't just stand there. Shoot him!"

"Can't," said The McGregor. "I left my bow in my tree stand."

Tulip, realizing there would be no help from The McGregor, shinnied back up the tree and squatted on the lowest branch, the long-johns trailing from his ankles, shivering mightily with his arms clasped about his chest.

The buck, perhaps angry that a paramour had escaped his lust, stalked the pile of scent-laden clothing; first slashing it with razor-edged hooves; then attacking it with its antlers; finally tossing the now-shredded garments into the air, panting and snorting in rage.

Meanwhile, The McGregor had retrieved his bow, nocked an arrow and holding the weapon at full draw, waited for the frenzied buck to settle down long enough for a clean shot. "Can't you do something to keep him from hopping around?" he called to Tulip.

"You want me to jump on his back and hold him f-f-for you?" Tulip stuttered, blue with cold. "S-s-shoot! Damn you! Shoot! I'm f-f-freezing up here."

When the buck heard the harsh human voice coming from directly overhead, it momentarily forgot its battle with the pile of clothing and lunged for the long-johns which were hanging off Tulip's ankles and flapping in the breeze below the branch. The sleeves tangled in the buck's antlers and Tulip hugged the tree trunk in both arms, holding on for dear life. Puzzled, the buck braced himself to gather strength to jerk at the thing that was holding its head, and that momentary hesitation was all The McGregor needed. He rolled the bowstring off his fingertips and the arrow penetrated the buck's chest cavity just behind the front shoulder, piercing the heart. The buck shuddered once and his legs sort of folded under him. As he fell his weight stretched the long-johns to their limit, yanking Tulip loose from the tree.

Calmly, The McGregor sauntered over to where Tulip, his unprotected body now scratched, bruised and bleeding, was struggling to pull himself from under the dead bulk of the deer. "You've got to hand it to Maynard," he said. "That *Rut* scent of his sure brings 'em in. This buck is a ten-pointer. I should win the Big Buck contest easy."

Tulip glowered at him, slipped the tattered long-johns off his ankles, struggled upright, took two purposeful steps, and hovered menacingly over The McGregor. "Any hunter who can jump from a tree stand to wrestle down a buck deer when the hunter is stark naked at the advice of another hunter deserves to put his tag on the animal, don't you think?"

"You stink," said The McGregor, looking up at Tulip's great bulk. "You really stink. And you still don't smell anything like your name."

They were laughing together when Mrs. Joyce Vandenberg and her husband Alvin walked up on them. The Vandenbergs had been out gathering nuts. If it weren't for that, this story would never have gotten out.

Simple Sustenance

*N*o roadside Greasy Spoon that I know of is harder on an outdoorsman's stomach than gathering and preparing your very own wild foods. I've been a woodsman all my life, and I speak from experience. For I've yet to come up with a foolproof way to identify the so-called wild edibles.

Indeed, I've squandered a mini-fortune on a wild foods library to no avail. It includes all the books of stalker Euell Gibbons; several sparse and allegedly informative volumes by Brad Angier; plus a recent work by a wild food addict with the unlikely name of Weiner. These remarkable works, for chapter after chapter, dwell on the merits of pigweed, mountain sorrel, and even cactus roots as the basis of a palatable and nourishing diet.

In addition, I've studied obscure doctoral theses hidden in the dank basements of several university libraries and once audited a wild foods identification course at Colorado's famous Aspen Institute without receiving a flicker of enlightenment.

Perhaps my lack of gourmandise when it comes to wild foods has something to do with an inherited defect in my spatial reasoning. For no matter how hard I try, I'm unable to correlate the precise line drawings usually found in wild food boods with their actual living brethren in forest and field, not to mention those found in mountains, prairie, swamps, deserts and river bottomlands.

All the books, for example, will tell you that poison ivy (*Rhus radicans* or *Rhus toxicodendron*, whatever) is a glossy trifoliate that no one can fail to identify. I cannot, however, so therefore I've avoided, since childhood, each and every plant associated with three of anything including clump birch (*B. papyrifera*).

Still, I acquire an itchy rash all over my body whenever I venture into the woods. Perhaps it is poison sumac I encounter; or burning

[143]

nettle. I don't know . . . the book plants and the on-the-scene plants never look the same to me.

I figured that the cattail was one wild food I couldn't miss on. Even I could identify *that*. So, following instructions in Weiner's book, I gathered the rhizomes of the species and proceeded to prepare them, precisely according to directions. (Cattail rhizomes are starchy tubers roughly equivalent to skinny potatoes.)

· The result was not a succulent wild food repast but a new Space Age glue (*Pat. Pend.*) which bonded anything to everything within moments. This discovery came about soon after my sticky rhizome concoction boiled over on the new electric range and stuck my wife's favorite copper-clad saucepan to the burner. It took fifteen minutes, a twelve-pound sledge, and a stout logger's wedge to bust it loose.

And I remember the time I fermented elderberry wine after I learned the fine points of winemaking in a non-credit night course at our local university extension. The instructor, a multi-degreed bacteriologist and presumedly knowledgeable in the ways of fermentation, suggested that his students age their squeezings in a warm place.

· I selected my furnace room.

Unfortunately, the good professor neglected to tell us that you must use thick bottles—I used throwaway soda bottles—otherwise the seething contents would soon build up a gas pressure sufficient to burst a thin container. My bottles didn't merely burst, they exploded, and the contents expanded like some alien froth in a horror movie and enveloped the gas furnace in goo.

Then, the suds gobbled up my winter's supply of food, both domestic and wild, that I had stored nearby. Hickory nuts, dried berries, vension jerky, salmon planks—all were engorged and ruined in the path of my bottle-busting elderberry wine.

The episode brought a bill from the furnace repairman of $69.34 to unclog the burners and rekindle the pilot light.

So much for the theory that you can cut the household food budget by collecting and processing wild ingredients.

I could go on to tell you about my experience with acorn flour (results akin to amoebic dysentery); the puffball mushroom adventure (a long vigil with a stomach pump in the local hospital); or the wild honey episode in which I tried to gather nature's gold from an immense wild bee tree (permanent Neanderthal browline despite the application of several bottles of calamine lotion).

[144]

But I won't . . . You wouldn't believe them anyway.

So I no longer care about the esoterics of gathering and eating wild foods, other than an occasional relapse which has me forage a few wintergreen leaves to munch while trout fishing or grouse hunting.

And I've vowed the next time I travel into the wilderness I'm going to pack an ample supply of peanut-butter-and-jelly sandwiches for simple sustenance . . . If I venture there at all.

Mayflower Farm

*N*orbert Archambault was a slightly built bantam rooster of a man. We called him Cubby and thought him a leprechaun.

Cubby and his sister, Anne, tended chickens and goats and honeybees on a backwoods North Country farm across a forty-acre field from my boyhood home.

Cubby was an environmentalist, although I didn't know it at the time —a precursor of a genus which would proclaim, three decades later, that its practitioners had the inside track on understanding what makes nature tick.

But Cubby Archambault loved to teach about natural things, and Mayflower Farm was his outdoor classroom. On weekends and as soon after school as we could sneak away from chores at home, the Sandberg kids were gamboling about Mayflower Farm as Cubby stoically taught us about how living things are dependent one upon the other.

I particularly remember Mayflower Farm in the spring. Then, on the first warm day that foretold of nature's annual reawakening, when the cowslips pushed butter-colored petals through the remnant patches of snow in the swamp behind the goat barn, Cubby would release the honeybees from winter hibernation.

Thus, the spring I was seven years old, I received my indoctrination in the age-old mystery of the birds and the bees. Cubby's tale was far different but no less intriguing than the similar story I would learn while frequenting Ma Zebrasky's pool hall a few years later. His was a simple recounting of what bees mean to nature, to birds, and to man.

"I know what bees mean to me," I recall saying to Cubby while innocently munching the sweet, waxy, comb honey he'd cached in an oaken barrel the autumn before.

"Yes," he said, "you know what bees make but have you ever wondered why or how they make it?"

Between sweet slurps I admitted that I did not.

And that's when I received my first lesson in ecology . . . at Mayflower Farm in the spring.

When Cubby released the awakening bees after taking the hives from winter storage in the stone basement of his "Honey House," he admonished us that in nature, nothing good ever happens quickly. It would take from now to the end of summer, he explained, for the bees to make another batch of honey.

First we skittered the hives across the dirt floor of the storage room and into the warming rays of the sun.

"Wait," Cubby said. "Wait for the miracle."

Expectantly, scrunched on our haunches, we peered into the tiny opening that was the access to the hive.

Soon, from deep within, a low buzzing sound rose from a murmur to a protracted hum.

The bees, Cubby said, were singing a hymn and asking the Pope to intercede on their behalf before they entered an unfamiliar world. The irreverence was typical. Although he was a devout Roman Catholic, his impish nature led him to mock ostentatious religious ritual and social mores.

In those days, for example, the regimen of the Church dictated that members abstain from eating meat on Friday. Cubby got around the restriction by declaring: "If you can't eat meat, eat chicken!"

As the first bee crawled groggily from the hive, those of us who had gathered for the coming-out party also came alive. For the emergence of that single bee meant the colony hadn't been affected by a too-cold winter. It meant, too, that we'd better move the hive to its summer place on the edge of the apple orchard before the occupants got too lively and explored the penetrability of the watchers' skins.

Quickly we carried the hives to the orchard. And by the time the last was blocked and leveled several more half-asleep bees were clutched at the entrances.

"Watch," Cubby said.

Then a venturesome bee decided, for some inexplicable reason, to fly away from its lodging into the natural world beyond. And thus progressed my first lesson in ecology.

I shall never forget it. First, Cubby led us on a merry chase after the

[147]

bee. "Where is it?" we cried, for the insect was soon lost to sight.

"The bee," Cubby said, "will be in the arbutus blossoms near the big pine tree."

And sure enough it was.

Then Cubby explained how you can understand what any creature will do in any circumstance if you've first observed enough of its habits to know what it wants.

This bee, he said, wanted nectar to make honey. So it had lit out to the nearest nectar cache—the patch of trailing arbutus near the pine tree.

Later, in midsummer, Cubby showed us how the bees, in their search for nectar to make the honey we'd eat next fall, would also gather pollen on the hairs of their legs and transfer it flower-to-flower, assuring that the plants would grow again next spring.

"It's a never-ending cycle," he said. "Bees help flowers and flowers help bees. If there were no bees and no flowers there would be no birds because birds eat seeds, the fruit of the flowers.

"And if the birds which have no food happen to be grouse or pheasant, you won't have them to shoot and eat during hunting season . . . and the Sandberg kids won't have full bellies."

Since, in those days, there was an abundance of wild game for the platter, I thought Cubby a little weird for carrying on the way he did.

But I understand him now.

At Mayflower Farm that spring, those many years ago, I learned about nature from Cubby Archambault, but more important perhaps, I learned about life.

Ghosts Along the Thunder

Big Ed fumed as another feathered grey thunderball boomed into the cedars, cleanly missed. As the grouse swung a hard left around a bushy white spruce, Ed adjusted his yellow-lensed shooting glasses and gazed at his favorite 20-gauge side-by-side with something less than affection.

"That's the seventh straight miss this morning," he grumbled. "These Thunder River grouse are either ghosts or I need new glasses."

I laughed at the outburst, for Big Ed didn't know how close he'd come to the truth.

We were hunting the Thunder River country, which offers some of the finest grouse shooting in the state, perhaps even in the nation. Big Ed knew the area well and is an excellent shot both in the field and on the skeet range. So it was understandable that he was peeved at his lusterless performance this fine autumn morning.

Suddenly, the steady tinkling from the collar bell that tracked Arna, Big Ed's proud and wide-ranging English setter, abruptly silenced.

Big Ed moved ahead of the point and *Boom!* a grouse hurtled from the thick cover. Then *Boom!* another ricocheted out of the trees.

I quickly downed the second bird, a tricky overhead shot. Big Ed triggered the first barrel when his bird hit fifteen yards and missed. Then he touched off the second barrel when the bird was straight-away at twenty-five yards and missed again!

"Damn!" he sputtered, "they've got to be ghosts. Not even Doc Faye would miss an easy shot like that."

"What's this about ghosts?" Doc Faye's booming voice surprised us as he crashed out of a nearby aspen thicket.

Quickly, I explained about Big Ed's problem with the elusive Thunder River grouse.

Doc listened quietly, peered slyly at Ed, and commanded in his best doctor-to-patient voice: "You better come into my office first thing Monday morning, boy. Sounds like you need new glasses. I've been telling you that the eyes always go before the legs. Those phantom partridge you've been seeing are nothing less than clinical proof of premature senility."

Big Ed grimaced and turned down the trail. "Time for lunch," he said.

"Haw, haw," Doc called after him. "Thought I'd heard every excuse there was for missing birds, but ghosts is just too much."

Doc Faye is an ophthalmologist, a specialist in eye diseases. Like many professionals who become interested in their vocation because of intriguing personal problems, Doc had been afflicted with poor eyesight since childhood. To overcome the handicap he wore heavy, thick-lensed glasses. And he is intolerant of any who are unwise enough to dwell on his affliction, even playfully.

A few weeks back, Big Ed, who should have known better, had inadvertently violated Doc's sensitivity. Doc had missed an easy crossing shot on a loafing woodcock and Big Ed teased him with a tirade that included the expletive "four eyes."

At that time, Doc's reproach had been unusually mild. But his furrowed forehead forecast that his agile mind had hatched the scheme he was playing out today.

"I'm going to teach that clod some manners," Doc had confided earlier in the week after asking that I drop by his office after work to discuss "something of importance."

"Recognize these shooting glasses?" he asked.

"They might be Big Ed's," I ventured.

"Almost duplicates," he cackled in reply. "But this pair is modified. Not enough to change his vision nor to be unsafe . . . just enough to throw off his aim."

I laughed long and gleefully. "Doc, I don't know if what you're about to do is a breach of ethics, but it's absolutely diabolical—I like it!"

"What's unethical?" Do retorted, grinning. "This is merely a scientific test to discover how a slight change in a lens prescription will affect shooting ability."

"Yes," I agreed, "and in keeping with your scientific scruples, the victim, I suppose, must be kept unawares."

"Exactly," he replied, "but the correct term is *subject*, not victim."

Doc slipped the bogus glasses into the pocket of Big Ed's hunting vest and hid the regular pair in the cluttered glove box when we stopped for breakfast. Earlier, we had agreed that we would tell Big Ed about the switch after we pumped a brandy Manhattan into him at George and Jane Schussler's Bavarian Inn on the way home. So far, the ploy had worked beautifully.

That afternoon, although Doc usually hunted alone so that he could proceed at his leisure, he suggested that we hunt as a trio. "I've got to see some of those ghost birds myself," he confided.

Arna ranged to the left of the logging road and Doc's Brittany, Patch, cast to the right. Soon Arna was firm on point. Big Ed pushed in for the flush and dropped the bird as quickly as it leveled.

"Luck!" Doc growled. "Pure, blind, luck!"

But after Ed dropped a second bird, then a third, and Doc had missed his first pair (one of which ruffled its feathers in defiance after fluttering to a roost in a tree directly over his head) Doc became perplexed and blurted, "How come these things were ghosts for you this morning and for me this afternoon?"

"Doc," Big Ed said slowly, "maybe you need shooting glasses. The yellow tint cuts the haze, you know."

Doc looked at him, surprised.

"Here," Big Ed grinned, "try these. I found an extra pair in the glove box of your car when I was looking for a pipe cleaner after lunch."

Intently, Doc studied the offering. "No thanks," he said. "Even a four-eyes like me can see that they're the wrong prescription."

Big Ed laughed.

Then they turned and tramped happily down the trail together in search of another ghostly Thunder River grouse.

A Place of One's Own

When the hard, icy winds of midwinter send thick windrows of snow across my driveway—so heavy that removing it from its usual repository in front of the garage door requires more energy than I care to expend—I feel the urge to hoard my possessions close about me. Perhaps you do, too.

By January, of course, the thunder of a ruffed grouse bursting from an aspen thicket, cleanly missed, is little more than a whisper. And the sound of singing waters at Camp One Rapids Pool, where a huge brown trout lurks, ever disdainful of my fly, is too far away in time to anticipate intensely.

It is now the in-between of more glorious seasons. And I am contented to conjure visions of a place, an inner sanctum, where I might escape the rigors of cold reality by handling, polishing, and gloating over those tools that bring a sportsman cherished moments: guns, rods, reels, shells in every weight and load, flies and lures in never-used abundance, and knives and packs and skis and game calls.

The problem is, at my house and likely also at yours, the tools are scattered—lack of space.

For example, my new 20-gauge over-and-under, which scored a double on grouse one warm and golden morning last October, is now tucked away in the hall closet between piles of wet snowboats and fuzzy-collared winter coats. And my favorite ultralight spinning rod, which last June throbbed a fighting Pine River brook trout to net, is waiting for the new season in the basement, buried between half-used paint cans and old newspapers.

My brier-scarred hunting coat, unlaundered since I acquired it several years ago and therefore irreplaceable, swings from a hook in the attic. And my waders, which need replacing, hang from a similar hook in the garage. Hopefully the cold will crack them deeply, be-

[152]

yond repair, so I've a reasonable excuse to buy a new pair in the spring.

"These things," I muse, "if assembled together in one place might help me while away the winter with vivid thoughts of pleasanter times."

But how?

Soon that simple question has inspired fantasy. My thoughts soar, performing long, lazy Immelmann turns in my mind.

Then chortling to myself I speculate: "Perhaps there *is* a way. The master bedroom is ideal. It's big and bright and airy. The tiny sewing room would serve for sleeping just as well. And the sewing room could be removed to the basement . . . if I get rid of the newspapers."

"What's that you're mumbling about?" my wife inquires.

"Nothing," I reply. "I'll tell you later."

So now, self-inspired by yearning, I begin to fashion my master plan for transforming the master bedroom into a place of my own.

My wife's closet, because it's larger, will be ideal for hunting gear. Except, of course, for the guns. They will be displayed in a fine walnut cabinet that will be custom fitted to the nook in the east wall. There, the setting sun will glitter off the oiled, blue steel and the mellowed wood of the stocks.

My closet, because it's taller, will be perfect for fishing tackle. I won't even need to break down the rods between seasons. I'll simply hang them from tiny screw hooks embedded in the molding near the ceiling.

In each closet, too, I can build neat little fold-out work-benches: one for the fly-tying vise in the fishing closet; another for the reloading tools in the hunting closet.

The space between the windows will be good for bookshelves to hold, near at hand, Burton Spiller's *Grouse Feathers*, Dana S. Lamb's *Where the Pools Are Bright and Deep*, Leopold's *A Sand Country Almanac,* Bergman's *Trout,* and all the other sporting classics that I'll be re-reading once I have a place of my own.

To read them in, I can buy that antique leather sofa and chair in the window of the Third Street Resale Shop—they're serviceable and cheap.

On the floor, of course, a full bearskin rug. (Hillard Selvey has one, also cheap, which his wife insisted must be removed from *their* master bedroom.)

The frilly curtains will have to go. They will be replaced with something more masculine—burlap perhaps. And for drapery hooks I can use those unfilled deer tags I've accumulated over many years. They will add a nice touch and also serve as a conversation starter for friends who visit here.

Nor will the room be completely decorated without a massive rolltop desk and a solid brass cuspidor.

I'll line the walls with trophies, too. Trophies that I don't have now but which will surely come . . . once I've a place of my own. For once secluded there, no detail of future hunting or fishing trips will escape my planning. No essential sure-fire fishing lure will ever be forgotten. Nor will any exotic quirk of game or fish go unanticipated.

How satisfying these visions are. How less burdened now my mind. As I build upon my whimsy, the drifting snow outside the window is not quite so foreboding as it was only minutes before.

Somehow it's become lighter, fluffier, more amenable to shoveling.

And October's ruffed grouse sound is back, bigger than life. The heartbeat flutter of the wings is louder now and the sound of the thumb-sized aspens clacking closed behind its exit is like all the chopsticks of China plucking rice at dinner hour.

I can visualize, too, clearly and intensely, the Camp One Rapids trout as it leaps silvered from the water. It's a gigantic leap that sails it over the shadow of the tallest white pine. And this time the fish does not reject my fly!

Still, one thing bothers me: the master bedroom is on the second floor. If it is indeed to be a place of my own it needs a great stone-faced fireplace where logs can crackle on a winter evening to warm my thoughts.

But how does one go about shoring up the second floor of a sixty-year-old home to accommodate something so massive?

First thing in the morning I'll ask Dick Nelson, my engineer friend, to look into the problem. He knows about such things.

Then, once he solves it, I'd better ask my wife what she thinks of the whole idea.

A Woodie for Duke

*T*he October dawn was lovely, too quiet for proper waterfowling, yet so radiant with promise that my with-it friend, Sam Bair, an addicted waterfowler now excommunicated by circumstance to a duckless corner of New Mexico, would have chanted if he'd been here, "Good vibes, Man!"

The open water of the beaver pond was covered with tiny spheres of duckweed. In the morning calm the surface resembled a nubby, green-tweed carpet.

Overhead, luminous scudding clouds of violet and pink formed a canopy for the pond as first light framed the treetops and awakened the resting mallards: *Puruck-puk-puk,* they called, saying "Good Morning" to each other.

I checked my watch: the time was nearing official sunrise—my prearranged signal to begin sloughing the backwaters of the pond.

As the two jump shooters for the morning's hunt, Jim Toth and I would get our shooting when the ducks spooked from the shallow puddles among the tussocks in the flooded sedgemeadow. These leg-grasping knobs of marsh grass and muck, common to flooded beaver pond everywhere, were interspersed with larger pools, cattail clumps, and alder brush islets.

Our tactics, devised to provide all the hunters fair shooting, would drive airborne ducks down the pond to Ray Gordon, who was hidden behind the four-foot-high beaver dam, and to Paul Lulinski, who was concealed in the brush on a slim point of land that thrust into the open water.

Paul is one of the best wing shots I've seen and Gordy is a close second. So they automatically became the stationary shooters for the day. And Jim and I, and Paul's brother, John, lesser shots by far, became the "jumpers." Tomorrow we'd rotate assignments.

As I stepped into the shallows, the shell ice shattered in the stillness and slowly I broke a pathway toward the nearest mallards, which were chuckling unseen behind a huge mound of vegetation—a muskrat's winter food supply.

The razor-hard ice sliced across my legs just below the knee. At every step the bottom muck worked to suck the waders from my feet. The tussocks of marsh grass, laced together with a meshwork of underwater roots and beaver cuttings, made tough going in the half-light. And so intent was I about proceeding quietly, that I was unprepared when the first small flock of a dozen mallard burst skyward from the pond.

I shouldered the over-and-under, but even as I pulled the triggers in succession I knew that I had misjudged the lead.

Quickly I reloaded.

Another small flock went up from behind some screening brush rearward of me. I twisted, shot, and missed twice more.

By now the air over the pond was a confustion of startled ducks, no two of which seemed to be flying the same direction. More than two hundred mallard were up. And there were pintail, blue-winged and green-winged teal, bluebill, gadwall, even a flight of black duck, rare in this area. Occasionally, a wayward wood duck would rocket low across the pond and straight into the trees.

I heard shots from the beaver dam and others from the point. I saw a fat mallard hen fold and curve downward on Jim's side of the pond. And then a greenhead flared from behind a cat-tail clump not fifteen yards from me. I waited until it was straining for altitude about twenty feet off the water, wings up, neck distended, and using very little lead I shot, missing again.

A few dozen yards to my left, well concealed in a natural blind under an overhang of bankside cedar, John, with his black Labrador retriever, Duke, had come off the pond to position himself where any birds that elected to follow one of their favorite escape routes along the shoreline to a gap in the trees on the tail of the pond would be easy targets.

I scanned the sky, saw no incoming birds, and waded through John's decoy spread to join him under the tree. Duke was lying sullenly nearby, his head cradled in his outstretched forepaws, rolling his eyes. It was strange behavior. Ordinarily the dog would have been sitting alertly at John's side.

"What's with him?" I asked, nodding my head toward Duke.

[157]

"He thinks that every time he hears a shot there should be a duck down on the water for him to retrieve. So far this morning he hasn't had any action. So he's sulking."

I looked at the dog, admiring, as I had many times before, his great size and powerful forequarters. At 110 pounds, from Canadian stock, he was one of the most massive black Labs I've seen. And he was absolutely crazy to retrieve waterfowl.

A day earlier, when we circled the pond after early morning shooting to pick up two cripples that had dropped into the brush at pondside, Duke had cold-trailed, found and retrieved both birds with ease.

One bird, a tough mallard drake, had crawled under the tangled thatch of a huge blowdown forty yards into the woods. Duke sniffed his way to the spot, inspected the perimeter of the snaggle of branches, crashed in, rummaged around, and came out carrying the bird, which was merely wingshot and squawking loudly.

"I swear that dog is almost human," I said. "You must be proud to own him."

"He is more intelligent than some humans I know," said John. "But I don't own him. He owns me."

"What do you mean?" I said, laughing.

"You'll see," John said. "If you hang around him long enough he'll own you, too."

Now, as I watched Duke studying us from the vantage point he'd chosen for himself, I could understand the dog's chagrin at being deprived of the opportunity to do what he most enjoyed—retrieving birds off the water.

"Well, John," I said. "I haven't done any better than you have this morning. Maybe it would help if we team up. That flight of wood ducks that buzzed us yesterday might be back today. The woodies probably like to set down to feed about the same time each morning."

"The way I'm shooting," John said dourly, "those birds don't have a thing to worry about . . . I've got the feeling there will be no woodie for Duke today."

We sat under the cedar, sipping coffee and munching on *Powerhouse* candy bars (as if the brand name would somehow improve our laggard skills) and listened to the cries of success coming from the direction of the beaver dam. Finally, I dozed.

[158]

"They're coming in," John whispered, awakening me. "I'll take the lead bird, you take the second."

The wood-duck flock came in from the east, directly out of the sun, low over the water. We crouched and waited as they made their first pass over the decoys, came around, and set their wings.

"Now!" John said.

We sprang into shooting position and our guns roared in unison, two shots each, the sounds echoing from the wall of trees on the opposite side of the pond. At the sound, the birds accelerated and zipped away, unscathed.

Duke, too, came alive at the shot sounds, launching himself into the pond with a single powerful leap. After hitting the water with a mighty splash, he came up immediately and swam in vigorous circles, his head high out of the water, swinging from side-to-side, scanning for birds.

Finding none, he spotted a length of wood, denuded by beaver, floating among the decoys. Paddling strongly and purposefully to it, he grasped it firmly in his mouth and paraded his find by swimming in furious, tight circles. Then, with what appeared to be disdain, he shook the stick savagely before tossing his head to send it arcing through the air in a trajectory that ended in a splashdown at John's feet.

"I think he's trying to tell you something, John," I said, laughing.

"Yes," agreed John, reaching down to ruffle Duke's head as the dog stepped from the water. "He's telling us that he has just retrieved the only kind of woodie he's likely to see today."

I shook my head, broke my over-and-under to check for shells in the chamber, and reached into my pocket for the shotgun's fold-up case.

Duke waggled his huge body, shaking out the water, which wetted John and me in icy spray, then stalked away to resume his place under the cedar. There he snuggled his head on his outstretched forepaws and rolled his intelligent brown eyes from John to me and back again.

And I saw that at that moment, Duke knew that I knew that he'd acquired another duck hunter for himself, albeit not a very skillful one.

Requiem for a Hunter

Old Joe Hallen and I lie stretched out under an unseasonably warm late-October sun after tramping miles of Northwoods logging road in search of a fleeting shot at a ruffed grouse.

In his seventy-four-plus years Joe had hunted this covert every chance he got. Perhaps it was sixty times; maybe even a hundred. He couldn't recall exactly. All he knew was that over the years it had always produced well.

But we wouldn't hunt it today—it was posted.

Joe eyed the shiny metal sign from our resting place near a huge spreading clump of stark-white paper birch just outside the barbed wire fence.

I was disillusioned. He'd told me of this place so often I'd anticipated that we'd need only to walk a few yards and grouse would spin out of the understory to fall to my gun like flies to a spray can of potent insecticide.

It wasn't to be. The metal "Keep Out" sign, bright yellow and recently implanted, warned us in foreboding black lettering: *This Property Leased to Flying Acres Rod & Gun Club. Violaters Will Be Prosecuted*. The notice was signed by a prominent Big City businessman from downstate.

"Shouldn't that say 'persecuted' instead of 'prosecuted'?" I grumbled.

"I saw this day coming for years," Joe sighed, pulling his wallet from the hip pocket of 20-weight wool hunting pants which had been worn down to 16-weight by years of hard travel in these woods. ". . . Been meaning to talk to you about it for quite some time."

Then he dug through an accumulation of old bills, photos, and miscellany to hand me a piece of stained and crumpled envelope.

"Hate to say 'I told you so,' " Joe said quietly. "But I'm doing just that."

I unfolded the tiny square of paper which, now that I recall it, he had offered to me reverently. It was aged yellow and carried in his wallet so long that it was nearly pasted together by grit, sweat and frequent soakings, perhaps from tumbles in the icy waters of his favorite trout stream. Faded, purple ink dated it as having been written September 19, 1921.

I read it slowly.

Old Joe waited.

"Well," he said impatiently, "what do you think?"

"I think . . ." I replied, ". . . I think you've said it all."

He smiled.

"When I cash-in," he said, "you make me a promise."

I nodded.

"You promise me to have those words carved on my tombstone . . . just like I wrote them. It will be my . . . my . . . how do you say it?"

"Epitaph?" I ventured.

"No," he said. "It ain't that."

"Requiem?" I tried again.

"Yes," he said, "it'll be that. But you do it."

I looked at Old Joe . . . at the evil yellow sign . . . at the faded words on the snip of paper carried in anticipation of this moment for many years . . . at the towers of cloud in the crisp autumn sky . . .

Then I quickly pushed myself from my seat beneath the birch, stuck the muzzle of my 20-gauge through the top and middle strands of barbed wire, and squiggled through the fence into forbidden territory.

"To hell with that tombstone, Joe. Let's make our own requiem right here. Let's hunt!"

"No," Joe said. "I'm too old for fightin'. You go in if you want to. It ain't worth it to me anymore. You go in; I'll sit here."

I climbed back through the fence, of course, for it's no fun to hunt alone. And as I did perhaps Old Joe saw the glistening in the corner of my eye. Because he creaked himself rather ungracefully from the carpet of fallen leaves, as old hunters are wont to do, and slung an arm clumsily around my shoulder.

"I seen this day coming," he said. "But I never thought I'd be around when it actually came. Won't be too long and the only way you'll be able to hunt this country is to pay for it. They been doing that in England and Germany for years."

Embarrassed now by unusual emotions, I couldn't bring myself to look at him.

Instead I gazed again to the grouse-filled covert beyond the fence, through the golden leaves of autumn, and then out, deep into the clouds and the crisp blue sky.

Old Joe knew them well. But I, by virtue of being born forty years too late, would never know the simple pleasure beyond the fence at all.

The thought hurt.

Old Joe clamped his arm tighter around my shoulder. "Walt," he stammered—affection was not easy for him—"they don't make land like this anymore. No . . . The good Lord don't make no kind of land anymore. That's why you and me can't cross this here fence. We've got to learn to live with progress."

And when old Joe said the word "progress" he spat it. A hard, quick sound like the fall of an axe when splitting an oak.

"Yes," he said, "the only way to live with it is to adapt . . . Been that way with life all through history."

With that, old Joe somehow changed. He straightened and what remained was defiance.

I watched him look around us, examining the fence . . . the forbidden covert . . . the trees . . . the clouds . . . the sky.

Then he looked back at me. He knew I was watching, too. He knew I was seeing, learning.

"Boy!" he commanded. "It's too late for me, but it's not too late for you. You've got to do something. If you don't, hunters like you and me are going to be as dead as those dinosaurs."

I nodded.

"And that's why," he said, "you've got to promise to put those words on my tombstone . . . so you'll remember."

We walked back to the car without a bird—without even one *shot* at a bird. Still, that day remains in my memory as the finest day of hunting I've ever experienced.

It will be several years, but when the time comes I'll have those words carved on Old Joe's headstone.

In the meantime, I think the message in them is so important that they should be first carved here . . . on these pages . . . so that all will know as Old Joe does and as I do now:

> *A time is slowly drawing near,*
> *when the mystic haunts of the white-tail deer,*
> *and the secret coverts for grouse, I fear,*
> *or the greenhead mallard's nesting year,*
> *won't even be remembered here.*

The Last Sentinel

*I*f you're like me there is one Christmas tree in your life that you remember well. Some special memory is attached to it; all your other Christmas trees have been forgotten.

My special Christmas tree is one which never graced our living room: a magnificent and perfect double-needle balsam fir that should have been cut, then adorned with care, one winter evening long ago, but was instead replaced by a sparse, lopsided spruce.

So my special tree still thrives, on a pine-scented island, deep within the marshy bottomland that separated the river from the sandy upland hills of my boyhood home.

I *know* my special tree still thrives because every now and then, over the past twenty years, I've visited the hummock to look at the tree and to wonder at my youthful astuteness in not having chopped it down.

In the meantime, that uncut tree has become for me . . . The Last Sentinel.

Sometimes, during my infrequent visits while hunting grouse in its vicinity in autumn, or while puffing after snowshoe hare in winter, the melancholy of it growing older is heavy on my mind. "When you go, tree," I ask, "will I go, too?"

For the tree, of course, is a symbol of my youth and it, too, is maturing, growing older—rusty needles on its crown—too rapidly for me.

And then I realize that the discolored needles, which come and are cast off every three years by most conifers, only symbolize aging on the balsam's top while the greying strands in my thatch are never lost but slowly and inevitably accumulate.

The tree, I sense, will be rusty-topped long after I am gone. And that disturbs me. Had I cut it and hauled it on a rope to our farm-

house living room those many years ago, perhaps it would not re-
mind me, now, that all things will someday end . . . even me.

That year—the year I did not cut the tree and therefore sometimes
now regret my sentiments—November came and left, dry and brittle,
a month so sad it could not easily be forgotten.

Then came December, brisk, fresh with new snow, and so in-
vigorating that it, too, is still remembered.

As the eldest of five kids it was my duty that year to select from our
forty-acre swamp the tree that would grace our living room on
Christmas Eve. And knowing that, I watched for a suitable specimen
all through my autumn wanderings.

Early in October, while chasing grouse from their nighttime covert
across the swamp, I found the tree—that perfectly shaped double-
needle balsam, then six feet tall.

My Tree, as I came to think of it, was growing on a sunlit hummock
unmolested by larger trees and was, therefore, precisely conical from
earth to crown.

It was beautiful. So beautiful that I took to walking into the marsh-
land each day after school just to admire it. And after each visit I
thought: "Wait till they see this tree!" For I had visions of how my
tree would become my claim to fame, my ticket to adulation.

On Christmas morning, I envisioned, the neighbors would drop
by, see my tree, and exclaim: "I've never seen anything like it. Magnificent!"

At night, I dreamed of how my tree would look when tinseled and
strung with the ornaments that my mother treasured in a protected
corner of the barn from New Year's Day until the following Christmas Eve. Ah, the accolades I would receive because of that perfect
tree.

But the more I visited my tree, the more I understood of it, the less
I wanted to cut it.

I saw, for example, that the ruffed grouse liked to nestle under its
low, overhanging branches when the weather was bad. And I saw
the red squirrels scamper beneath it, nipping at its tiny cones.

There was a robin's nest, too, halfway up the crown. And cottontail hid beneath it when the grouse weren't there.

Then there was the crow, always perched on the spire, that scolded
me for intruding into its world.

Once, I saw a white-tail deer munching on the tender, pale-green
needles, my tree's "young of the year."

And several times I saw the red of a cardinal flash away at my approach. There were always chickadees flitting about, of course, and bluejays and deer mice and other tiny woodland creatures.

Spiders loved to spin their trailers from the lower branches to the hazelnut bush on the sunset side. And I watched insects become ensnarled in the sticky web and saw how the spider stalked along this stealthily laid and deadly pathway to engorge its tangled prey.

So when the time came to cut this magnificently lovely, conical tree, I could not.

Instead, I selected a scraggly spruce so sparse of limb that few wild creatures called it home. It was deformed on one side because it grew hard against a huge, shadowy red oak.

But, I reasoned, the flat side would conform to the corner of our living room, which it did.

Then, after Dad had finished tossing tinsel—he didn't believe in hanging it strand by strand, but he lobbed it from afar for a more "natural" effect—I was happy that I had not cut my tree. For the lopsided spruce was passable and the neighbors dutifully admired it on Christmas morning.

Today, when I venture afield in autumn, I always stop a while, on that marshy hummock, to look upon my tree, still perfectly conical, and now more than twenty feet tall.

"When you go, tree," I muse, "will I go, too?"

In response, a cardinal flashes from the branches, a crow scolds from the spire, a red squirrel chatters . . .

And I know, of course, that my tree will outlive me, a self-created immortality, of sorts . . . My Last Sentinel.

Can anyone have more?

PART III

. . . to Burnt Stump Lodge

The Creating of Kalibusch Cannibus

*H*illard Selvey leaned back in his chair, pulled nervously on an ear with his thick, stubby fingers, and peered through the glare of the gas lantern that hissed above the red-and-white checkered tablecloth. "You guys sure look glum," he commented.

"Don't we have good reason to be?" Howie Peterson moaned. "We can't fight those developers. They're too big and they have too much money."

"I don't agree," Hillard responded. "That real estate bunch may have power downstate, but I think they can be beaten up here. There's got to be a way . . ."

"Fat chance!" Howie retorted.

As unofficial chairman of Burnt Stump Lodge's unofficial board of directors (the "board" included anyone who owned, used or visited the old log cabin) Hillard had hastily summoned the others to a meeting at their Northwoods retreat after receiving his mail copy of the local weekly newspaper.

And although it was a work day, a majority of the board had traveled to the meeting, sliding down the rutted tracks to the shore of Parton Lake just after a thundershower.

Indeed, some had taken time off jobs to get there; others had driven more than two hundred miles from their homes.

"Read that article to us again, Hillard," Big Ed suggested after the group had settled around the table.

Hillard nodded and picked up the newspaper, tilted his head to focus the print through his bifocals, then cleared his throat by coughing pretentiously.

"The headline says," he began," 'Downstate Developer Plans Vacation Village on Parton Lake.'

"And then it says:

'Real Estate Investment Corp., an investment group with offices throughout the Midwest, announced today that it had formed Wilderness Shores, Inc., to develop a recreational complex on Parton Lake. Construction is scheduled to begin early next spring.

'According to Carter Graham III, a spokesman for the firm, "when completed in the early 1980's the development will include six, 100-unit high-rise lakeside condominiums, more than two hundred single-family rustic vacation homes, a campground, a marina, a convention center, an olympic-sized swimming pool, and a nine-hole golf course."

'Graham said the company has already secured options for most of the twelve hundred acres needed for the project, including more than five thousand feet of frontage on the northeast shore of Parton Lake and more than one mile of the South Branch, a Class I trout stream which flows through the site.

' "Unlike many developments," Graham said, "this will be a class operation. It will proceed with due regard for the pristine nature of the Northwoods environment."

'Graham explained that a "central sewage plant adequate to accommodate a population of 3,500 permanent residents and 6,000 transients is planned and all utilities will be underground." '

"That's it," Hillard sighed, taking off his glasses and pulling nervously on his ear.

"Listen to that," Big Ed scoffed. ". . . due regard for the pristine nature of the Northwoods environment. With all those people coming in, there goes the trout fishing on the South Branch."

"Yes," Howie agreed. "And there goes the deer hunting, too. My stand is on the northeast shore . . . Probably smack dab in the courtyard of one of those high-rise condominiums."

"We could offer to buy them out," someone ventured.

"That's about all we could do . . . offer," Howie replied. "None of us has that kind of money. We wouldn't have it even if we pooled our savings."

"What we need is an endangered species," Big Ed volunteered.

"A what?"

"An endangered species. If an area is home to a plant or an animal that's on the endangered list, nobody can develop it."

"Now you've got it!" Hillard said excitedly. "That's the answer. I told you there was a way."

"Got what?" Howie asked dourly.

"I read where a group in Maine," Hillard elucidated, "stopped construction on a big power dam after somebody discovered a colony of endangered wild snapdragons called furbish louseworts."

"Furbish louseworts? You've got to be kidding."

"No," Hillard continued. "And an obstructionist group in Tennessee stopped construction on another dam after someone discovered a minnow, called it a snail darter, and had it declared an endangered species . . . after the fact."

"You mean . . ." Howie sputtered, " . . . you mean we should invent an endangered species to stop Carter Graham?"

"No," Hillard replied. "Not invent. *Discover!*"

"You know that little fluorescent-green beetle that shows up in the South Branch every August," Jimmy, the youngest of the Burnt Stump directors spoke for the first time, ". . . the one we imitate with a Green Jassid? I took a specimen to my entomology professor and he said he'd never seen anything like it."

Big Ed laughed. "I think you've got it, Jimmy. If those folks in Maine can have a snapdragon, and the Tennessee people can have a minnow, I don't see why Burnt Stump Lodge can't have a beetle."

"But how can we say it's endangered," Howie countered, "if the professor couldn't even give it a name?"

"Well . . ." Hillard said tentatively, "if we discovered it, I expect we're entitled to name it."

"Yeah," Big Ed agreed, "but the name should be catchy so it sounds good on TV. A Latin name perhaps."

"How about *Kalibusch cannibus?*" Jimmy suggested.

"Sounds good," Hillard said. "But what does it mean?"

"I don't think it means anything," Jimmy responded. "It just sort of popped into my mind . . . probably something I remember from a nursery rhyme."

"Sounds like a kind of marijuana, to me," Howie interrupted. "That's all you college kids think about nowadays."

"Whatever it means," Big Ed interjected. "I like it. It sounds scientific and also has a nice ring."

"I don't know," Howie speculated. "That Carter Graham must be a pretty smart person. What if he doesn't go along with it?"

"He may not go along with it," Big Ed reminded him. "But the

[171]

boys at the state department of natural resources and at the federal Environmental Protection Agency are just itching to identify more endangered species so they can build bigger empires. And until Graham and his bunch can prove otherwise our beetle is endangered and the bureaucrats won't allow Graham to start construction."

"Exactly," Hillard added, "which gives us plenty of time to think up another angle. We can drag this out for years."

"It's getting late," Howie reminded them.

"So it is," Hillard replied. "Let's have a vote. All in favor of making the endangered green beetle of the South Branch *Kalibusch cannibus* signify by saying 'aye.'"

"Motion carried," Hillard smacked his hand down hard on the tabletop to the chorus of agreement.

Then he picked up the newspaper, crumpled it into a ball, and dropped it into the fireplace where it burned with a pleasing yellow flame.

The Poltergeist Musky

"*I* had that big musky on again this morning," Howie Peterson said. "He tore everything away on the first run—lure, line and leader, a cable leader and 20-pound-test line on a light drag!"

"Yeah, Howie," we said, for we'd heard him lament the loss of this particular fish several times before.

"I'I know what you guys are thinking," Howie fumed. "But there *was* a fish . . . a big one . . . probably the next state record."

"Sure, Howie," we said.

"What Howie did," Big Ed needled, "was hook the same underwater snag every time he trolled over that so-called hot spot. I'll bet he's never actually seen that fish."

"No," Howie admitted. "But it can't be a snag because it always peels off my line before it breaks away."

"I had that happen to me one time," Hillard Selvey observed, "when my line got wound around the prop."

"Maybe that fish is a poltergeist musky," Hardwood Hansen suggested.

"What's that?"

"A fun-loving spirit fish that enjoys tricking fishermen, particularly those who stretch the truth."

"O.K." Howie sputtered. "I get the message. You guys will never believe me until you can go after him yourselves . . . Right?"

"Right," we chorused.

"He hangs out near the pickerelweed off Buzzard's Point, on the shallow side of the deep hole."

Trying to conceal our excitement, we merely nodded at Howie's information, for learning where a musky lurks is half the battle in catching it.

Trophy musky tend to establish feeding territories in the best locations in any lake. They find a suitable lair and patrol from there. It's the underwater equivalent of the lion's den. Any angler lucky enough to identify the location of a territorial musky has a good chance of taking a better-than-average fish sometime during the season if he fishes the area often. For the mere fact that the fish has taken over one of the limited number of homesites in a lake means it is strong enough and ferocious enough to fend off the advances of dozens of other fish who wish to stake out the same lush feeding and breeding empire.

"I think I'll try for some bluegill," Hillard yawned casually and slipped out the cabin door.

"I'm going after some bass," Big Ed noted as he followed Hillard to the pier.

"I'd like some perch for supper," Hardwood added as he sauntered after the others.

"Wait a minute," Howie cried. "You're not going after *my* musky without taking me along."

Soon, the three boats were trolling around the pickerelweeds on the shallow side of the hole off Buzzard's Point. But after two hours of fishing, the mini-armada had managed only two medium-sized northern, nothing more. No one got so much as a follow from Howie's monster musky.

"Howie," Big Ed declared, "if I find out that you've been putting us on, I'll tell your wife about the time you . . ."

"I swear this is where he hangs out." Howie was agitated. "Maybe he's just off feed. Let's have lunch and try again in mid-afternoon."

Grudgingly, Big Ed agreed.

That afternoon the big fish sucked in Hillard's black bucktail on the first pass. Quickly the other anglers reeled in to watch the action which, as it turned out, was brief.

After engorging the lure, the fish rolled once on the surface and then charged toward Hillard's boat, streaking under it on a straight-line route to mid-lake. In seconds, it had peeled Hillard's line to the spool and *Ping!* it was over.

"Did you see it?" Howie said excitedly. "I told you guys he was the next state record."

All of us had seen the fish, of course, and it was huge, no question of it. But we'd seen something stranger, too. When the fish rolled on the surface after slamming the bucktail, the water had cascaded off shiny flanks that were bone-white in color.

The strange fish and its powerful run held our conversation through dinner at George and Jane Schussler's Bavarian Inn.

"Did you see that musky's eyes?" Howie asked. "They were red and cruel-looking . . . like there was blood in them. He must get mad as hell when he's hooked."

"Yeah," Big Ed agreed. "And he actually *charged* Hillard's boat. He really did!"

"It was his color that I can't get over," Hillard said. ". . . Ghost-white. Maybe he *is* one of them poltergeist musky Hardwood was telling us about."

"Excuse me," a diner at the next table turned toward us, "but I couldn't help overhearing. I'm the area fish manager and I can assure you that the fish you had on is real. He's been tearing up our test nets for years. I sure wish you had boated him."

"Is he big enough to beat the state record for musky?" Howie could barely contain himself.

"Any angler lucky enough to catch that fish will have a new state record, all right," the fish manager said, grinning. "But not for musky. The fish you had on is one in a million. Probably a shortnose gar, weighing over a hundred pounds. And we're fairly sure that it may be a near-albino, which accounts for its unusual white color and pink eyes."

Rocking Chair Doe

No matter how hard we tried, there was no way anyone could get the edge on Uncle Henry.

Still, we wanted to catch him in an indiscretion and persistently laid traps for him. Our maneuvers merely spurred Uncle Henry to fabricate taller and more outrageous tales which, after he retold them a few times, became unassailable fact in his mind.

Once, on a fine September weekend, Burnt Stump Lodge was crowded with members and their guests. Some were here to bow hunt for white-tail deer. Others wanted the last two days of stream trout season to pay off with a trophy brown. Still others had come to enjoy the unsurpassed fall musky fishing on the nearby lakes.

"I've decided not to go trout fishing this weekend," Uncle Henry had informed us the night before.

"Why not?" one of the trout anglers inquired, for he knew that Henry preferred fly-fishing for trout above all other outdoor pastimes.

"All the good-sized browns left the South Branch and took off for the main river when their favorite food died off."

"Oh?" said the angler, interested now. "What was that?"

"Three-pound crickets," said Uncle Henry, smiling slightly and characteristically rubbing the white stubble on his chin.

Instead, Uncle Henry went musky fishing on Saturday morning. And just before lunch he was back at the cabin, fishless.

The trout fisherman he'd conned with his cricket story happily displayed his catch—a creelful of above-average brown trout. "Henry," the trouter needled him, "I hate to see a man get skunked. I'll share these with you if you like."

"I didn't get skunked," said Uncle Henry indignantly. "I had a fish on that was so big it reminded me of one of those mini-submarines the scuba divers use."

"That so," said the trout fisherman, thinking he had finally gone one-up on Uncle Henry. "I suppose the fish parted your line like it was sewing thread and swam away."

"No," said Uncle Henry. "My line held. It was high-test monofilament—brand new!"

"Then how did you lose the fish?"

"Didn't lose it."

"Then where is it?"

"Well . . . ," said Uncle Henry, knowing the trout angler was deeply hooked, "that musky was so huge it scared the daylights out of me. I didn't know what would happen if I hauled it into the boat."

"So?"

"So I cut him loose," said Uncle Henry.

"You're putting me on."

"No, sir," said Uncle Henry, stringing the hapless angler along. "And that isn't the half of it."

"There's more?"

"You bet. When I cut him loose that musky was one angry fish, let me tell you. He was so mad he charged the boat."

"What happened then?"

"Well . . ." said Uncle Henry, "when he opened his mouth and chomped down on the transom with those ugly yellow teeth, I thought I was a goner. I can't swim, you know."

"He actually chewed on the boat?"

"He nearly engulfed it! Ripped a hole in the fiberglass the size of a pit toilet. I could have swamped in a minute."

"Come on now. If the fish bit a big hole in the boat and you can't swim, how come you're here to tell about it?"

"You won't believe this," said Uncle Henry, "but the electric trolling motor was running at top speed when the musky hit. He must have thought it was a giant *Mepps* spinner. And as soon as the whirling prop ticked his jaws he spit with such force that the boat beached ten yards inland of the water."

After lunch Uncle Henry declared that he was still so shook up by the monster musky "nearly eating the boat" that he would spend the remainder of the day relaxing on his bow-hunting stand. He'd scouted the area a week earlier, he said, and knew where an over-sized white-tail doe did her afternoon feeding.

"She's old and fat and past her fawn-bearing prime," he explained. "But she's as big as a two-year-old Jersey cow and should

[177]

make good eating. She'll be tastier than those sex-starved bucks the rest of you are after. They've worked off all their tallow running down some lovin'."

Upon overhearing the remark, the trout fisherman smiled and said, "At least we won't need to listen to Henry's tall tales this evening. Deer of any kind are scarce this year. He won't see a thing."

"Wanna bet?" Hardwood Hansen joined the conversation. "Uncle Henry always sees *something*."

When Uncle Henry returned from this hunt you could tell he was quite pleased with himself. The sun had just dipped below the treeline and a golden autumn day had become crispy satiny twilight thr.ugh which we saw the merry glistening of Uncle Henry's eyes.

"How did you do, Henry?" someone asked.

"I saw that doe, all right," he replied. "She was even larger than I remember her. She had a rack on her as big as a rocking chair. But I didn't even draw my bow."

We looked at him quizzically and I knew what each of us was thinking: *Uncle Henry has finally slipped up. A doe with antlers?*

But Uncle Henry hesitated only momentarily before arcing his arms wide overhead to show the spread of the doe's antlers. Then, without another hint of perplexity, he continued: "Yup. She had a rack on her this big. Must be one of those mutants you sometimes read about. Let me tell you, I've never seen anything like her before during all my years in the woods."

The Producers

"Why don't we get shooting like that?" asked Howie Peterson as he watched the celebrity host of *American Outdoors* take his second double on grouse during the course of the half-hour television program.

"Simple," Big Ed said dryly, "they piece the good film together and throw the bad stuff away."

"Yes," Hardwood Hansen agreed, "and notice how those TV sportsmen only go out in perfect weather."

"That's so they won't ruin their make-up," someone observed.

After three days of steady, pounding rain which had ruined bird hunting for the weekend, the Burnt Stump hunters were becoming saturated with card playing and television viewing. Now, their inactivity had bred the first symptoms of cabin fever. Some were irritable, others giddy, and one or two had already entered an advanced catatonic stage of boredom in which they did nothing but stare at the cabin wall.

"I wonder if that television character really took that pair of doubles on the same day," Howie Peterson interrupted the silence.

"Maybe he didn't take them at all," Big Ed suggested. "It could be a camera trick. Those birds were coming in at odd angles."

"It's all an illusion," Hillard Selvey added. "I once read an article about how photographers get those great wing shooting action shots. Sometimes they hide caged birds in the grass. When the dog points the birds, the shooter steps into position, an assistant pulls a string to open the cage, and a spring-loaded device actually throws the birds into the air. *Whammo!* The cameraman gets some beautiful wingshooting film."

"Another technique," Hillard continued, "is simply to toss a dead bird into the air ahead of the gunner. Just as the body starts a downward arc, he shoots. If the camera is aimed at the proper angle, it will look like an actual kill on film."

[179]

"Why don't we do that?" said Howie.

"What?"

"Make a film of us taking doubles on grouse. If we show it at the conservation club meeting, we'll be celebrities, too."

"Yes," said Big Ed. "I'll bet we could even make some money on it by selling it to the TV station."

"We could make bigger money if we sold it to several TV stations. Syndication, I think it's called."

"Why don't we do it?"

"For one thing," Hillard said, "sound movie equipment is expensive. For another, none of us knows the first thing about movie making."

"I have a friend at school who works parttime for the college public relations department," Jimmy, the youngest of the Burnt Stump hunters offered. "Maybe he could borrow their equipment and also be the photographer."

"That's it!" said Howie. "All we would need to do is buy a roll of film. I can see it now: the movie opens showing me taking a double on grouse, then the credits come on . . . Produced and Directed by Howie Peterson, Created by Howie Peterson."

"Who said you could be the star?"

"It's my idea, isn't it?"

The rain temporarily forgotten, the hunters gathered around the table and talked excitedly about their project. After much discussion, they decided the film had to show each of them taking a double on grouse. Howie would be listed as the producer because it was his idea. Hardwood would be the director because he knew where to find the grouse. Big Ed would be the special effects person because he was the tallest and strongest and could throw the dead birds the farthest. Hillard would be the dog handler because his English Pointer, Belle, was the best grouse dog. And Jimmy would be listed as the assistant cameraman. The title of the movie, of course, would be *Doubles on Grouse* and the closing credits would list it as being presented by Burnt Stump Films.

Early the next Saturday, Jimmy arrived with his cameraman friend whose name was Freddie. Freddie had a pony-tail tied up with a string of love beads, the wisp of a beard, and wore a large gold earring in his pierced, left earlobe. Hardwood looked at Freddie with distaste, then directed the group down a logging road and into a small meadow that had been seeded in clover. "This is a good morning feeding ground for grouse," he explained. "The clover draws them from hundreds of acres around."

"I've already taken some nice close-up shots of grouse," said Freddie proudly. "It was easy."

"Where did you take them?" Hardwood asked suspiciously.

"Right next to the cabin while I was waiting for you guys to come out. Look! There's one now." Freddie pointed to a large gray bird which fluttered on a branch in a nearby spruce tree.

"That's not a grouse. That's a Canada jay. Don't you know what a grouse looks like? Haven't you seen one before?"

"I've never been in the woods before," Freddie admitted. "I was born and raised in Chicago's Loop."

"Listen to that," said Hardwood, imitating Freddie's rather singsong voice and casting a scathing look toward Jimmy. "Freddie has never been in the woods before."

"He's a fine cameraman," Jimmy defended his friend. "He won a prize for a program he filmed about the college ballet troupe."

"Ballet!" sputtered Hardwood. "My God!"

"All that matters is that he knows how to use the camera," Big Ed interrupted. "Besides, the way ballet dancers flitter about isn't so much different from the way a flushed grouse moves."

Hardwood frowned at Big Ed and ordered gruffly, "O.K., Freddie. Set up your camera across from that stand of aspen near the bend in the trail."

"Ah . . . what's aspen?" Freddie asked.

"That bunch of skinny trees with the yellow leaves."

"Oh."

"When you see the dog stop near the trees," Hardwood continued, "get ready to film because in all likelihood a grouse will fly out and you can get some good footage of me dropping the bird."

"You drop a bird?" Big Ed needled him. "That I've got to see."

Hillard walked Belle toward the aspen and three birds, wary from the commotion perhaps, burst from the trees before the dog had a chance to go on point.

Two of the birds, screened by the aspen, rocketed directly into the swamp. The third elected to escape down the middle of the road and flew straight toward the hunters at shoulder height.

"It's attacking!" Freddie screamed as the grouse flew toward him. Then, just as the bird collided with the camera, Freddie covered his head with his arms and dove into the roadside ditch. The grouse,

[181]

momentarily stunned, walked groggily in circles before flying off into the trees.

"Did you get that on film?" Hardwood was excited. "That was a once-in-a-lifetime action shot. We'll probably never get another chance to film the flight of a grouse coming head-on like that."

"When . . . when . . . that . . . ah . . . thing attacked me I didn't have time to turn the camera switch," said Freddie.

"He wasn't attacking you. He was merely flying down the road."

"Now what?" Big Ed inquired as he spewed a stream of Red-Man into the brush.

"We'll shoot a bird and you can do the special effects tossing," Hardwood replied. "That is if Freddie isn't frightened of dead birds, too."

Several yards down the road, Belle bumped two grouse out of heavy cover and Hillard managed to down one with an easy overhead shot.

"Freddie," Hardwood explained, "when Belle retrieves the bird, get a shot of her just as she walks out of the brush."

"Find, Belle, find," Hillard directed the dog. But Belle sat down in the road, scratched her ear with a hind paw and yawned.

"Should I start shooting now?" Freddie asked.

Hillard grabbed Belle by the collar and dragged her into the brush. The rest of us watched while strange sounds emanated from the woody tangle. Once, we heard Hillard cuss and demand: "Drop, Belle, drop." Soon, feathers floated out on the wind and drifted over the road.

Finally, Hillard crashed out of the maze, followed by Belle, who was licking her muzzle, bits of grouse down sticking to her lips.

"Hurry, Freddie," Big Ed was laughing, "get some film of that."

"I'm out of film," said Freddie.

"Out of film?" Howie was surprised. "How could you be? You haven't shot anything."

"I've been taking mood shots."

"Mood shots?"

"Yes. Trees, sky; you guys walking down the road . . . things like that."

"And you used up all our film?"

"I only shot one reel."

"You mean you need more than one reel?"

"Of course. To get enough footage for a half-hour show we'll need to shoot ten or fifteen thousand feet."

"How many feet in a reel?"

"Four hundred."

"My God! It will cost a small fortune. Why didn't you mention that before?"

"You guys said you'd supply the film. I thought you'd know how much we'd need."

"Gentlemen," Hillard said, "I think it would be wiser if we squelched this project and left the celebrity status to Curt Gowdy."

"Yes," Hardwood agreed. "And if *American Outdoors* ever needs an experienced cameraman, I know where they can hire one . . . cheap!"

Four of a Kind

*H*owie Peterson stamped the snow off his felt-lined boots on the door sill of Burnt Stump Lodge, walked stiffly to the fireplace, fanned his hands to catch the warmth from the hearth, and muttered to the cardplayers seated around the table. "I can't understand it," he fumed. "Two years ago snowshoe hare were bouncing around these woods like dandelion fluff in a tornado. And all I saw today was a set of week-old tracks."

"It's the bottom of the cycle," Hardwood Hansen commented as he pushed a nickle into the growing pile of coins on the table. "It's an example of the supreme imbalance of nature."

"Imbalance?" Jimmy questioned. "My biology professor always calls it the *balance* of nature."

"Just goes to show you how book learning tends to pervert reality," Hardwood responded dourly. "When you've been logging in the North Country as long as I have, sonny, you learn that the natural state of nature is disharmony. There is no single balance of nature. There is an infinite number of possible ones. Nature is on the end of the teeter-totter, not perched in the middle. She's either swinging up or swinging down."

"Let's get on with the game," Big Ed interrupted. "The kid didn't ask for a lecture from some grizzled old coot whose only purpose in life is to separate us from our poker money."

"That's all right," Jimmy said. "The professor told us all about the timber barons. She explained how they see nature only as something to chop down, dig up, or shoot. 'Exploiters,' she called them."

"Timber baron! Exploiter!" Hardwood smacked his huge, work-scarred fist on the tabletop. The impact rattled the coins in the poker pot, causing several to roll to the floor and drawing the ire of the other players.

"See how those academic know-it-alls are brainwashing our

[184]

youth?" Hardwood fumed. "Next thing you know the kid will be mouthing platitudes about how we hunt just because our rifles represent phallic symbols."

"What's that mean?" Jimmy inquired.

"Look it up in the dictionary," Hardwood bristled.

"It's the politicians." Howie walked over to the table and rested a booted foot on a nearby chair to undo the laces. "They appeal to the big-city voters by promising to lock up the North Country in wilderness. That way they don't have to explain why there aren't more natural areas near population centers. The last governor was a real-estate millionaire. Another big-money man is a prime candidate for governor this election. And a majority of the legislature and bureaucrats are attorneys who get fat fees on the side by closing real estate deals. Those people don't want to promote small natural areas near big cities because it would deprive them of the loot they knock down by speculating in suburban land."

"Gee," Jimmy said. "I never thought of that before."

"There's a lot you young wise-guys haven't thought of before," Hardwood smirked. "And I'll give odds that your professor friend spends time up here on vacation."

"How did you know *that?*"

"Simple." Hardwood pointed a knobby, walnut-hued finger at Jimmy. "The people who most want others to be deprived of their lands and their livelihoods are those who won't lose anything. They want large tracts of wilderness somewhere other than where they're at. That way they can make quick trips from the city and see big trees and herds of wildlife without having to get out of their air-conditioned gas guzzlers."

"The professor drives a small foreign car."

"Worse yet," Hardwood grumbled.

"It's the politicians," Howie repeated. "All their talk about preserving wilderness for future generations is a smoke-screen for their land deals."

Hardwood ignored Howie's outburst, preferring to counsel Jimmy. "I don't argue the need to preserve representative samples of wilderness for scientific study," he elucidated, "nor am I against preserving one or two large tracts in each region of the country. But ask any city dweller what wilderness is and he'll describe an outdoor circus such as Yellowstone where the bear beg Fritos at roadside and where there's a lavender flush-toilet at the end of every path."

[185]

"I'm beginning to understand," Jimmy said, not wishing to further provoke the sage of Burnt Stump Lodge.

"Then there's hope for you yet," Hardwood replied. "You might even come to understand that the word 'resource' means 'an available supply which can be drawn on when needed.' God put trees and wild creatures on this planet for man to use. All he requires is that we use them prudently. If we don't harvest them, the resource is wasted. And that, to me, is the ultimate exploitation."

"It's the politicians," Howie muttered. "Anybody can see that."

"Let's play cards!" Big Ed was exasperated. "You guys are three of a kind. All you ever talk about is the woods."

Hardwood glanced at him, smiled and reached for his cards. After studying the hand for a moment with a great show of concentration, he dropped the cards face up on the table, fanning them to show an ace of each suit. "Make that four of a kind," he chuckled.

"Timber baron!" Big Ed sputtered. "Exploiter!"

Jimmy laughed.

Hunter's Ball

Hillard Selvey led the deer hunters of Burnt Stump Lodge into Bouncing Betty's Woodland Inn late on the opening Saturday of white-tail season. Once inside he paused to study the chaotic scene with an amused smile. The annual Deer Hunter's Ball was in progress, no doubt about it.

"Some dance," he grunted. "Nothing but red tuxedos. How are we going to take care of young Jimmy, here?"

The others snickered, beginning an evening-long charade that had been inflicted on first-time Burnt Stump deer hunters for nearly thirty years. And Jimmy, although he didn't know it, was to be the punchline for their joke.

"By the looks of this crew," one of the hunters commented, "Friends of Animals can rest easy. Not many of these dudes will see the woods at daybreak tomorrow."

"Yeah," Hillard said, "we'll just have a couple, then leave. O.K. with you Jimmy?"

Jimmy, just turned 18, nodded. He wasn't sure how he was expected to handle himself among the veterans. And they enjoyed embarrassing him by telling how they had once changed his diapers before burping him over a shoulder and popping a pacifier into his mouth.

"Hiya, boys," Bouncing Betty's greeting never changed. "What'll it be?"

Betty, somewhat unkempt, decidedly overweight and dumpy, sported a frizzed coiffure the consistency of starched spider web . . . She was a Northwoods legend.

For tonight's celebration, she wore a red wool shirt, striped bib overalls, and glossy spike-heeled shoes. As another concession to femininity, she had layered her face with stark-white pancake

[187]

make-up. The *coup de grâce* was brilliant crimson lipstick which struck off here and there around her mouth into the ghostly expanse of powder.

"How're things going this year, Betty?" Hillard inquired.

"Losin' money every day," she replied. "And unlucky for you booze went up ten dollars a case last Tuesday."

The hunters laughed, for it was well known that Betty inflated her usual prices as least one-third during the deer season.

"I'd like to introduce you to Jimmy, my nephew," Hillard said. "He's new this year."

Betty looked at Jimmy, fluttered her eyelashes, and drooled, "My, ain't you a sweet young thing."

Jimmy cringed.

The introduction had been Betty's cue to spike the newcomer's drinks and to ply him with exaggerated adulation. It would prepare him for the spoof which was to follow.

"I've never known her to shine up to anyone so quickly." Hillard nudged Jimmy in the ribs with an elbow. "She seems to like you, boy."

"She's . . . she's . . . old enough to be my mother," Jimmy sputtered. "My *grandmother,* even!"

An hour later, the overburdened drinks and Betty's attentions had taken a toll. "She's a real nicsh lady," Jimmy slurred.

Two rounds later the other hunters slid Jimmy's body off the stool, folded it into the car, and trundled him off to the cabin. The fun was about to begin.

Betty turned over her section of the bar to a sober patron and nosed her pick-up truck onto the icy highway to follow the Burnt Stump hunters.

"This won't take long," she called.

The crowd around the bar had watched the proceedings through-out the evening and many wanted to see the action, too. Soon an entourage of assorted vehicles bumped down the rutted trail to Burnt Stump Lodge.

The hunters, after undressing Jimmy's prostrate carcass, tucked it into the bunk. A lone gas lantern lighted the scene. The onlookers clustered around the frosted windows and speculated about the out-come. "The kid looks smart," one said. "This five-spot says he won't fall for it."

"I'll take that bet," a dozen others chorused.

Betty, still wearing her red wool shirt, bib overalls and spike-heeled shoes, snuggled under the covers beside the powerless victim and pretended to be asleep, snoring raucously.

"Ready?" Hillard asked.

"Ready," Betty answered.

Then Hillard shook Jimmy roughly by the shoulders. "Grab your socks, boy. It's daylight in the swamp. Wake up and let's get hunting."

It was only midnight, of course, but Jimmy had no way of knowing that. Groaning, he opened one bloodshot eye, then the other. "You guys go without me," he croaked. "I think I'm sick."

Then he noticed that he hadn't been sleeping alone. Gingerly, he reached over and pulled the old wool army blanket from the face of his snoring bunkmate.

"I didn't," he said, pale and bewildered. "I couldn't of . . ."

Whereupon Betty stretched from her feigned sleep, rubbed her eyes and chortled, "You sure did, sweetie."

"Gawd!" Jimmy moaned and passed out cold.

"Well, fellas," Betty said as she bounced out of bed. "We've initiated another one. Now back to the ball. One round on the house."

She knew she could well afford the goodwill gesture, for she'd just assured the Woodland Inn a steady business for the duration of this hunting season and a cadre of big spenders of next year's hunter's ball.

Stalking Snow

*T*he first big snowstorm of the season swept down from Canada and into the North Country late Friday as six-hundred-thousand hunters marshaled on the highways impatient to reach their favorite stands before the opening of white-tail deer season at dawn, Saturday.

On the six o'clock news, the TV weatherman recounted the storm's advance with that sadistic delight common to media meteorlogists everywhere. "It's a real Saskatchewan Screamer," he chortled, enjoying visions of atmospheric calamity. "More than six inches of snow should accumulate before morning and the temperature is expected to drop to ten degrees behind the passing cold front."

"What a jerk," Axel Abelman said as he punched the "off" switch on the TV set and turned to collect his hunting gear. "The drive north is going to be pure hell."

"Well," I said, "we'll have that tracking snow everyone has been hoping for."

"Tracking snow! What a misnomer," sputtered Axel. "A slight dusting of the stuff is all that's needed to separate a deer from its background. *Seeing* snow, I call it. Anything heavier is superfluous, redundant and absolutely unnecessary."

"Call it what you like, Axel," said Hillard Selvey, "but I'll be content if it's *getting-back* snow. You won't get lost when you can backtrack your own fresh trail."

"Oh, yeah?" Hardwood Hansen questioned. "How come I found you stumbling out of the brush way over on Zinther Road last season? There was plenty of getting-back snow for you to backtrack that time."

"Ah," Hillard replied. "How was I to know that some citified hunter had got himself lost while wearing boots identical to mine? Besides, the wind was blowing and covered his tracks."

I laughed, but I didn't join their banter because I had a plan for the next morning that would get me a trophy buck. And I relished the thought of the thick covering of tracking snow that would guide me to him. But that was before I learned that human hunters aren't the only creatures who will use fresh snow to stalk their quarry.

During the night the storm subsided and daybreak brought a dull sky of tarnished silver that subdued the woods and transformed the vast expanse of North Country around Burnt Stump Lodge into a bizarrely sinister world of disquieting stillness.

Overnight, the wet snow had accumulated on the tree branches, bowing them under the load. Then, with the sudden temperature drop the TV weatherman had predicted, the weighted boughs had frozen into grotesque disarray, sprouting phantom-like through the icy mist that shrouded the forest in ghostly white gauze. The effect was enchanting, but bewildering. The landmarks that had become familiar to me while chasing grouse around these hills in October were now out of proportion and mostly unrecognizable in the billows of low-hanging, ice-crystal mists locally called a "whiteout."

I should have known better than to blunder cross country at such a time, but the trophy-taking plan had been building in me since last deer season and now I was compelled to carry it out.

After knotting a bandanna around my neck as a barrier to the frozen snow that would plop from any disturbed branches to lodge behind the collar of my hunting coat, there to send trickles of chilling meltwater down my spine, I struck off from the cabin.

First, I explored the sharp, oak ridgelines to the west that the white-tails used as a nighttime feeding area. From there, I skirted the edge cover between swamp and uplands and then I wandered toward the beaver pond along the bank of an intersecting creek.

I was looking for the track of a buck. And once a likely track was identified, I intended to follow it and walk the animal down. It's a hunting technique that sometimes pays off in a handsome trophy but it can take the better part of a day. That's why most hunters don't attempt it.

You have to get an early start, too, if you're to locate a likely track before the fresh snow becomes marred by other tracks that could divert you from the trail. Then you work the animal fast and hard until you jump it from its daytime bed. After that you ease off and doggedly pursue it until your quarry becomes confused. Usually,

[191]

that will require five or six hours of methodical hounding after which the buck will become puzzled and unwary.

Then, as the animal realizes that its pursuer is a relentless cuss, it will become dazed and uncomprehending, stopping often to study its stalker. Such behavior is a signal to adjust your pace so that the deer will always be about a hundred yards away. Sooner or later, this will force the buck to stand its ground in a bold attempt to confront its tormentor. That's when you shoot.

Hardwood Hansen had indoctrinated me in this method, cautioning that its chief disadvantage is that I might have a dead animal on my hands, miles from the cabin with no clear idea of where I'd been nor where I was.

Still, my mind was made up. I would stalk a trophy buck this season and skid it back to Burnt Stump Lodge in triumph.

Now, as I wandered toward the back end of the beaver pond on the crackling new ice, I saw where deer, just minutes before, had munched on the greybeard moss that clings to the desiccated snags of tamarack and cedar that had been drowned in the rising water when the pond was formed. Evidently the moss was a delicacy, for I saw where the deer had walked directly to it over the still unsound ice.

Cautiously, keeping well away from the tree trunks, brush clumps and from the mounds of vegetation that were the muskrat's winter cache of food—all places where the ice was still dangerously thin—I studied the lacework of freshly laid deer tracks.

Although it's difficult to tell the sex and size of a deer merely by its tracks, Hardwood Hansen had shown me how careful observation will disclose a variety of clues. Taken together, the signs will help a hunter to discern the track of a trophy buck from that of a lesser deer.

Any small track, of course, can be disregarded. And a doe, even a large one, walks with a mincing daintiness. The imprint of the toe will be close to, and point forward or slightly inward of an imaginary line centered in the track. The mark of a doe's hindfoot, too, will be nearly superimposed on the impression left by the forefoot.

A large buck, however, walks purposefully, regally. Its tracks will be spread several inches to each side of the imaginary centerline, the toe will point outboard, and there will be a space between the imprint of the hindfoot and the forefoot. Generally, the larger the track, the farther the impressions from the centerline, and the greater the space between hindfoot and forefoot, the larger the deer.

The single track I came upon as I walked an open area of the thickest ice left no doubt that it was that of a trophy buck. The toe of the wide, splayed hoofs pointed outboard, spread ten inches on either side of the centerline, with a gap of perhaps six inches separating the tracks.

Quickly, I moved out along the trail. By its meandering course, I could see that the buck was unconcerned. It had paused here and there to nibble on the white cedar and hemlock boughs pushed down to within feeding height by the weight of the snow. Then, a few hundred yards from the pond, I came upon a patch of urine, yellow in the snow, still steaming.

I increased my pace, sure that my trophy would be bedded down only minutes ahead, and momentarily noted the eerie silence that had now become pervasive. It was a quality of the outdoors that I'd encountered only twice before: once, preceding a tornado; and

[193]

another time in the moments before a boar black-bear had slipped out of heavy cover to the bait below my bow-hunting tree stand.

A similar mood settled around me now; the soft swish of wool, the rhythmic crunch of snow, and the harsh rasping of my breathing as I walked were the only sounds. Still, I gave all of that no more than a passing thought, the image of the buck wandering about only minutes ahead firmly in my mind.

Indeed, so intent was I on the track that I was startled breathless by the flight of a snowshoe hare, mottled brown-and-white in its transition coat, bounding from a brushy, snow-covered burrow at my passing.

Later, a pileated woodpecker gave me a start when it burst from a head-high hole in a gigantic dead poplar tree, brushing my cheek with a wingfeather in its haste to be away.

After a while, the buck led me on a convoluted route into country that I had never seen before; as Hardwood had warned, I had no idea of where I was.

The increasing coldness of the air working against the warmth of the moist new snow had intensified the whiteout. Visibility in the woods was down to a few dozen yards. There was thunder in the distance, too, unusual this time of year, signaling the approach of another storm.

Near noon, I realized that the buck hadn't bedded down. Either the unsettled weather was spooking it, or perhaps I was traveling so closely behind that it didn't want to chance the rest.

By now, too, I was very thirsty, and hunger sounds gurgled in my stomach—ransom for my forgetfulness in having left my canteen and lunchbag on the table back at the lodge.

About mid-afternoon, the woods around still shrouded in the whiteout, as the buck again circled and crossed an earlier track, I was startled to see a third set of imprints along our backtrail. They were large, cat-like, with traces of fresh blood in every second pawprint on what would be a quadruped's left side.

"Cripes," I muttered aloud. "I've been stalking the buck and something else is stalking me."

At the sound of my voice I heard hissing sounds from up the trail, like the periodic escape of steam from a household iron, only louder. I turned quickly, saw nothing and uneasily resumed the hunt.

Light-headed now for lack of water and from too long without food, I began to speculate about the nature of the creature that apparently prowled this territory with me.

The Indians of the area, I recalled, often told tales of the Windigo—superhuman, evil giants, cannibalistic monsters with hearts of ice whose spirits arose in the deep forests in the dead of winter. It was said of them that they hissed at every breath and that their footsteps in the snow were always soaked in blood. And they were alleged to crave human flesh and to prefer dispatching their victims by disembowelment.

The idea, I decided, was absurd. Anthropologists have established that although the ancient Indians did see strange visions hovering among the ice-locked trees, and truly believed them to be a living Windigo, the spectres were merely hallucinations brought on by dehydration and lack of sufficient carbohydrates in a sparse winter diet.

Perhaps, I reasoned, the same illusion was now being created by my own mind for the very same reasons. Perhaps I'd only imagined the bloody tracks. And if that was the case I was near my physical limit and it would be wise to end the hunt and return to the food and warmth of the cabin.

But where was I? And where was the cabin? I had no way of knowing. The compass would not help. I hadn't used it to check my progress and therefore couldn't know in which direction the cabin lay. There was only one prudent thing to do: backtrack the trail. If I pushed hard, I should reach the cabin well before dusk.

I turned, ready for the long trek back, when I heard again the hissing sounds. Then, fifty yards of plodding along the backtrail, I saw where the bloody pawprints, perhaps at the time I chose to abort my hunt, had cut away and into a thick stand of cedar well away from the trail.

Wary now, I peered into the snow-covered boughs, trying to penetrate the maze, saw nothing, but was suddenly struck with the sensation that whatever had been tracking me so diligently was watching now, awaiting my confusion, ready to pounce at the proper moment.

I squatted to examine the bloodied snow. What I saw on my fingers was blood all right. It was no illusion. The creature wasn't a phantom. It was alive, probably wounded, perhaps by a trap. And it was hungry, although patiently stalking its prey.

"Well, my friend," I called into the cedars, "here's one supper that you shall go without."

[195]

In reply the hissing sounds resumed, accompanied by a nervous rustling from deep within the screen of trees.

Then, glancing up, I saw the buck, upwind of me, pawing in the snow with a forefoot and watching me curiously from atop a small hammock not twenty yards down the trail and midway between me and the stand of cedar. He was a magnificent animal and had obviously reached the point of distraction that I'd earlier hoped would be produced by my hours of steady pursuit.

Then, beyond the distraught and unsuspecting buck, I saw something more. A huge cat-like creature leaped soundlessly from the cedars, favoring its left forepaw. And cutting in from either side, forming a phalanx that would prevent the buck's escape, two smaller cats emerged, their maltese coats glistening in the pale golden glow of diffuse light passing through the icy mist.

The trio, which from my recall of all the animal books I'd read might have been outsized bobcats, converged in a few powerful and effortless bounds toward the deer. I watched, fascinated.

Too late, the buck sensed the attack. The middle cat was already on the deer's back, gripping the tawny hide with it talons, chewing at the buck's throat.

The buck, momentarily knocked off balance, screamed, reared, flailed the air with its hoofs, and whipped its antlers in a frenzied attempt to dislodge his attacker. The second cat blindsided the buck and the third cat dashed in to rip open the exposed belly with one powerful swipe of a paw.

The battle was over in seconds and the smaller cats tore into the buck's intestines, gulping the bloody, steaming tendrils with savage relish.

During the brief attack, I had remained, transfixed by the display, in my squatting position beside the trail. Now I slipped the rifle sling off my shoulder and stood to aim at the wounded cat—the largest of the three. But as I did so, the creature turned, bloody shreds of flesh clinging to its muzzle, and stared directly at me. I held the cat's gaze in my rifle sight for long moments, peering deeply into its penetrating yellow eyes, and I swear it was mocking me. For it dipped its head, curled its lips into the semblance of a conspiratorial smile, purposefully tore out the buck's heart, then tossed it skyward, catching it in midair and swallowing the meat in a single gulp.

I should have felt revulsion, or at the very least a measure of fright.

But I felt neither. It was as if some primitive signal had passed between us—predator-to-predator—that mutually acknowledged which of us was the better hunter.

I lowered my rifle, slung it on my shoulder and turned to trudge the backtrail to the cabin through the new-fallen stalking snow, as the thunder, closer now, resounded fitfully about me.

Talking to the Trees

"*T*hose balsam trees we planted on the northwest-forty sure look scraggy," Howie Peterson said. "But I'll have to bring one home as a Christmas tree this year so I can prove to my wife that the money we spent for seedlings has paid off."

"It's the soil," Hardwood Hansen said. "It's too sandy and too alkaline. Balsam need wet, acid soil to do their best."

"It isn't that," Big Ed interrupted. "Those trees are scrawny because we haven't paid attention to them. We just stuck them in a hole five years ago and forgot them."

"You might be right," Hillard agreed. "I saw a television science program a few weeks ago that said plants need companionship to thrive. They interviewed some scientists from California who showed how one group of corn plants grew four times faster than another group when they spent time talking to them."

"Corn plants in California aren't balsam fir in the Northwoods," Howie scoffed.

"True," said Hillard, "but the theory is the same."

"What have you got to lose, Howie?" said Hardwood. "If you want to stay out of trouble with your missus, you'd better have a good tree to show her. Why not try it? Select a tree and talk to it. Since it's only April, there's plenty of growing season left."

"If you guys think you can con me into talking to some stupid tree, you're out of your's."

But the other Burnt Stump hunters, knowing how naive Howie was, were sure that he'd been hooked. They were certain of it when Howie remained pensive and thoughtful throughout the evening. And when he announced, shortly after breakfast the next morning, that he was "going hiking," Hardwood, the best woodsman and the stealthiest stalker of the group, agreed to track him.

Deviously, Howie started his hike by walking into the woods in a southeasterly direction, away from the balsam plantation. Then, when he was out of sight of the cabin, he circled toward the northwest on a roundabout route.

Hardwood, once he saw what Howie was up to, walked cross-country directly to the plantation and hid on a knoll overlooking the area.

Howie lurched out of the undergrowth, nervously glancing over his shoulder from time to time, and studied several of the trees. Finally, he selected one of the healthiest specimens, sat down near it and appeared to be conversing with it. Hardwood, holding a hand over his mouth to stifle his glee, slipped away to tell the others.

"We were right," Hardwood reported. "He bought the crazy deal. He's out there right now actually talking to a tree!"

On the weekends that followed, each of the hunters reinforced the scheme by casually inserting odd bits of information into their table talk about how plants have feelings.

Once, Hardwood told of an article he'd read about a law enforcement lie detector expert who used his machine to show that plants, like people, become agitated when threatened.

Another time, Hillard told of reading a book which proved that plants have ESP—extrasensory perception—which enables them to tell if nearby humans truly care for them. "The book explains that plants are just like dogs," said Hillard. "They have some chemical in their cells that allows them to receive and interpret the slight electric impulses emitted by human brain waves."

Howie simply smiled, said nothing, and shook his head. But he continued to take his solitary hikes. No one bothered to follow him, of course, for they were sure of what he was doing.

"Howie, you never used to be so keen about physical fitness," Big Ed needled. "What made you suddenly decide to get into hiking?"

"Doctor's orders."

The others snickered but didn't press him for a better answer.

Then, in early July, when Hardwood returned to the cabin after fishing a secluded stretch of a nearby trout stream, he passed near the plantation, and curiosity drew him to visit Howie's tree. He was amazed. The tree had grown larger. It was symmetrical and well filled out, much greener than the surrounding trees.

"You should see it," he raved to the others. "That tree is damn near perfect. Maybe there is something to that mumbo-jumbo about plants having emotions."

"We've got a problem," Hillard declared on hearing the news. "We may have gotten ourselves into big trouble. If Howie brings a perfect Christmas tree to his wife, how are we going to pass off our dumpy ones on our families? We'll look like pikers."

"We could buy our trees from a commercial grower," Big Ed suggested.

"It's almost impossible to find balsam fir these days," Hardwood reminded him. "That's why we planted our trees, remember?"

"Maybe we should cut Howie's tree and blame it on vandals," someone said brightly.

"No," said Hardwood thoughtfully, "that would be cruel. We'll just have to select a tree for ourselves and start talking to it. There's plenty of growing season remaining. If each of us spends twice as much time with our trees as Howie does with his, it seems reasonable to me that we could catch up."

As the August weekends came and slipped into September, the comings and goings at Burnt Stump Lodge were marked by moments of slapstick comedy. They couldn't let Howie know what they were up to, for if he found out there would be no living with him for years; he'd see it as a victory over powerful forces and himself as the underdog hero.

Promptly, they devised a schedule listing who would have "Howie Duty" for each hour of every weekend. The duty person's job was to keep Howie occupied while the others were out talking to their trees, for when several of them were chanting in the plantation at the same time, the adjoining woodlands resounded with the din. The sound could be heard for some distance and evoked, in any who heard it, visions of a conclave of Hindustani gurus palavering on a mountaintop.

By late September, after days of unseasonable warm weather interspersed with soaking rains, a few of their trees appeared to perk up. But none matched Howie's in color, shape or in the lush density of foliage.

The contrast merely spurred them to visit their trees more often and chant longer, for it was unthinkable that Howie, a perennial worry-wart, fatuously innocent, should beat them at their own game.

At the close of the November deer season, as was traditional at Burnt Stump Lodge, the trees were cut. When lined along the cabin wall awaiting a burlap wrap to protect the branches on the long trip home, the magnificence of Howie's tree made all the others look like wilted Boston ferns.

"Sure is a nice tree you've got, Howie," Hardwood mentioned fitfully as they examined the harvest. "Where did you find it?"

"In the plantation, while I was hiking."

"Howie," Big Ed blurted, "we know you've been talking to your tree since April."

"Haven't you fellows been talking to your trees, too? . . . Since about July?" Howie responded blandly.

"Yes, we have," Hardwood confessed. "But your tree looks so much better than any of ours."

"Well," said Howie, "there is something that I've been doing that the rest of you may not have thought of."

"What's that?"

"First, you've got to do more than talk," Howie pontificated. "I've shown my tree that I truly love it by hugging and kissing it several times during every visit."

"You . . . you . . . hugged and kissed a tree?"

"Sure," Howie acknowledged, reveling in their discomfort, "and I did more."

"You did more?"

"Yes," said Howie. "Each time I visited my tree I also gave it a two-quart shot of liquid fertilizer."

Phantom Buck

*I*t passed my stand in the brass-colored frostiness of Opening Day as everyone said it would—a magnificent twelve-point white-tail buck, stately and powerful.

"You'll see him for sure," the veteran hunters from Burnt Stump Lodge said when they spotted me on a stand called The Knob. "Each of us has . . . and we've all missed."

"Come on, now," I scoffed. "You guys have been coming here each season for, let's see . . . fifteen years? Twenty? And you say it's the same buck? No white-tail lives *that* long."

"It's the same buck," they chorused. "You'll see. He has a white blaze on his forehead."

Since I've always enjoyed the metaphysical part of hunting—the part I don't always understand—I was eager to see the animal although I suspected the Old Timers might only be pulling my leg.

To watch the trail the buck would need to travel from his nighttime feeding area on the scrub oak ridgelines to his daytime home in a dense lowland cedar swamp, I had to squint into the remnants of a blizzard. For it had snowed hard through the night. Not the fluffy, silent flakes usually associated with the first tracking snow of the season, but tiny, diamond-hard needles that were driven now before a strong northeast wind. So I blinked constantly to wipe away the cold-caused tears.

Perhaps that is why I did not see the deer until it materialized in an opening among the popple trees midway up a steep hogback opposite my stand. I blinked, and wraithlike he was there, majestic and seemingly unwary.

Then, as he turned his great antlered head to study me, I saw the white blaze on his forehead. There was no mistaking it.

Entranced, I held my breath against his scrutiny. It was a mistake. For his image swirled away in a snow-laden gust of wind.

[202]

Late in the morning, as the veterans backtracked the trail for noon lunch at the lodge, Hardwood Hansen, the first to reach me, clambered up The Knob and demanded: "Did you see him, boy?"

"Yes," I said, describing the brief encounter.

"So you missed him," Hardwood said quietly. "You had him in your sights and you missed him."

"No," I confessed. "I didn't even pick up my rifle."

Hardwood laughed. "That was the phantom buck, all right," he said. "He'll do that to you."

On the second day of the hunt I was settled on The Knob well before daybreak. Again, as yesterday, just as first light paled the eastern ridgeline, I saw the buck. But today he had company—a sleek, nervous spikehorn.

I shouldered the rifle and watched the pair meander along the game trail. The larger buck held slightly in the lead, the spikehorn's head bobbing at his shoulder.

I aligned the crosshairs of the four-power scope to take the big buck low in the rib cage. Then, just before he stepped over the edge of the shallow ravine that would screen him from my view, I held and squeezed.

The recoil of the rifle popped my head from the stock and I lost the sight picture momentarily. When the scope steadied, I saw the body slide into the ravine leaving a trail of blood, brilliantly crimson, in the drifting snow.

"I got him!" I cried, although no one was about. "I've killed the phantom buck!"

Elated, I ran off The Knob to where the buck lay dead. And in the flashing luminosity of daybreak I saw, not the massive trophy I expected, but the spikehorn.

Upon seeing the body, I was struck with a singular feeling of finality that soon descended to self-recriminating doubt.

Had there truly been a trophy buck? Had I only imagined him? Had I simply *wished* him there?

If that was the case I had no business hunting.

But further inspection showed two sets of tracks in the snow: a heavy set with wide, splayed hoofs and a smaller, sharper set. The larger track continued on from where the spikehorn lay. The spikehorn must have lurched forward, shielding my trophy in the instant between my trigger pull and the bullet's impact . . . At least I think that's how it happened.

[203]

For I've never again seen the massive white-tail with the peculiar mark on his forehead, although other Burnt Stump hunters say they have.

So still I wonder: was the trophy truly a phantom? Or was he only an illusion created by the anticipation of the hunt and the tall tales vividly retold each season by the Old Timers of Burnt Stump Lodge?

A more reasonable explanation might be that the animal I saw, and the animal others say is still seen today, are descendants of a breed of super deer. This particular branch of the white-tail family may possess remarkable sensitivities which render them adept at detecting danger well before it can do them harm. And the white blaze might be hereditary and common to the clan.

But if that's the case, why is it that we never see a spikehorn nor a forkhorn similarly marked?

Maybe, as one veteran member of the party has suggested, the peculiar white blaze is a phenomenon of age which strikes deer ranging in this area—in human terms the equivalent being the premature white hair that affects many people of Scandinavian lineage.

Or perhaps, as all the other hunters say, the regal creature is, indeed, a phantom.

I don't know.

But it's possible the mystery can be solved in the brassy frostiness of Opening Day this November. I aim to try.

The Last Hunt

"*B*ig C's got me," Hank said quietly as we sat before the stone fireplace in Burnt Stump Lodge talking about the opening of white-tail deer season the following morning. "It's chewing up my insides."

"Big C? You mean . . . ."

"Yes. Cancer. Doc Bridenhagen gives me six or seven months. I'll never see another deer season."

"Come on," Hillard Selvey said incredulously, "you look healthier than any of us. Maybe they loused up the diagnosis. Things like that happen, you know."

Hank shook his head. "No, it's been confirmed . . . by specialists. Fortunately I contracted a virulent kind that acts quickly."

"How can you say *that?*" Big Ed was dumbfounded.

"Well . . . I figure it's better to have the quick kind than the type that will make you suffer for years."

"You can't really mean that," Howie Peterson interjected. "It's downright morbid."

"Perhaps it is," Hank replied. "But what else can I do? I'll tell you one thing, though, after I thought about it a while I saw it as an advantage. It's sort of pleasant to know precisely when you're going to go. That's more than the rest of you can say."

"Yeah, Hank," Hardwood Hansen said. "You know *when* you're going but you don't know *where* . . . and that's the important thing."

Hank smiled. "I've taken care of that . . . my immortality . . . in my will. I've directed that my body be cremated and that next opening day you guys will scatter my ashes near my deer stand here at Burnt Stump Lodge. And just to make sure you carry out my wishes,

[205]

I've added a party clause. When you get through scattering there will be enough money for you to hold a very liquid wake."

"You can't do that to us," Howie Peterson protested.

"I already have," Hank said, laughing.

More than three decades earlier, Hank Kreghoff had been one of the group of young World War II veterans who had built the log cabin on the shore of Parton Lake which was to become known as Burnt Stump Lodge. They'd axed down the virgin cedar in a nearby swamp, squared the logs by hand with an adz, and lifted the cabin walls into place with block and tackle. They were proud of their handiwork and enjoyed being with each other in the best white-tail deer country in the North woods. And Hank hadn't missed a deer hunt here in the thirty-four seasons since.

As the years passed, several of the original group of Burnt Stump hunters died. Some from war wounds, others from age. Their places were taken by sons, sons-in-law, and grandsons. Now, Hank was Burnt Stump's link with the past. For today's group of hunters, unlike the first crew, all of whom had lived within a few miles of each other, were scattered over the state and seldom visited between their annual hunts. And although it was a varied group—a carpenter, a football coach, a college professor, a timber cutter, a journalist, a scientist, a chef, a wine salesman, and an unemployed bartender—for these ten days each year each felt at home in their closed society; they were the "Boys from Burnt Stump Lodge."

"Boys," Hillard Selvey said. "Since this is Hank's last hunt I suggest that we forsake our individual hunting ways tomorrow morning and all pitch in to get him a trophy buck. If we station Hank at the junction of Stoney Ravine and the South Branch, the rest of us can converge toward Hank's stand and drive every white-tail deer in these woods directly to him. He might even get a shot at that twelve-point swamp buck we've seen in the creek bottom."

"No," Hank said. "I don't want that. I don't want to do anything differently this year than I've done in the past thirty-four. I'll hunt my usual stand tomorrow and take my chances with the rest of you."

"That doesn't make sense," Howie sputtered. "You haven't filled your tag in three years. If this is your last hunt why not make it memorable."

Hank grimaced.

Over the ten days of the season, all the Burnt Stump hunters, including Howie, made several silent drives daily toward Hank's stand, hoping to scare the big twelve-point swamp buck within Hank's shooting range. But darkness on the final day found only three deer hanging on the meat pole outside the cabin. None was Hank's.

Now, as the hunters loaded Hillard's station wagon for the trip home, Hank walked out of the woods with his octagonal-barreled Winchester—a birthday gift from his father—and announced: "I've decided to stay on here a couple of days . . . just to relax and look around. Maybe I'll try some early ice-fishing for walleye on Birch

[207]

Lake, or build some brushpiles for cottontail. I might even split a few cords of firewood for next season."

When Hank said "next season" the hunters acknowledged his words with a nod and turned away, embarrassed.

But Howie Peterson asked, "Sure you'll be all right, Hank? Maybe you shouldn't stay here alone. Not in your . . ah . . . condition."

"For gosh sake, Howie!" Hank said, annoyed.

Then, shaking his balding head from side-to-side and chuckling to himself, Hank walked to the open doorway of the cabin where he turned to wave good-bye. The fire crackled on the hearth behind him and fluffy flakes of cotton snow settled slowly earthward, sparkling when they drifted through the square of light.

"See you around, Hank," Hillard Selvey called before he rolled up the driver's side window and turned the key to start the station wagon.

"See you around," Hank echoed. "And Merry Christmas."

Then Hillard backed the wagon to the country road and turned it west toward the highway. But on the long ride home, unlike the boisterous trip which had brought us to Burnt Stump Lodge ten days earlier, we passed the miles in silence. No one spoke a word. Not even Howie.

EPILOGUE

January 1, 2000

The Sportsman's World is changing, changing fast. What will that world be like ten years from now? Twenty? On New Year's Day, 2000, will we look forward to the coming outdoor year with the same pleasant anticipation we felt for 1960, 1970 or 1980?

If, for example, someone had told you twenty years ago that to qualify for a chance at a single Canada goose this year you would need a state small-game license, a special federal waterfowl stamp, a special state waterfowl stamp, plus a special tag obtained by tossing a special license stub into a computerized lottery with those of several thousand other hopeful hunters, how would you have reacted?

But all of that has come to pass—and more. What new constraints, both necessary and frivolous, will be placed on hunters, anglers, backpackers and campers between now and the turn of the twenty-first century?

We can make some predictions.

It's certain, for example, that there will be more of us; population in this state will probably increase by more than 1.5 million over the next twenty years.

And we'll be living longer. Average life expectancy will be eighty-four years.

Most of us will work past age sixty-five, too, trying to make ends meet because of the limitations placed on retirement income by a depleted social security system.

Still, we'll have more leisure time to enjoy outdoor activities. Some of us will be working four-day weeks of 32 hours. Others will be working "flextime" hours—selecting which 8-hour stretch we wish to work in a daily 12-hour period.

We'll make more money than we do today. Average yearly pay will be $35–$40,000. But we won't be much better off—50 percent of it, against 37 percent today, will be withheld to pay for a burgeoning government bureaucracy. In 2000, one out of every five Americans will work for government, against one in six today.

These additional tens of thousands of bureaucrats will need something to keep them occupied, of course. Ideal makework projects will be administrating the gun-registration program, taking reservations—perhaps *years* in advance—for visits to national and state parks and campgrounds, and manning the permit booths that will control the handful of us who will be allowed to wander in wilderness areas or to go boating and canoeing on public waterways at any one time.

The future for one of these, gun ownership, is easiest to forecast, although other outdoor activities will be adversely affected by regulations, too.

By 2000, the "forward" thinkers in Big Government will have invented a legal way to obviate our constitutional right to keep and bear arms. Private ownership of handguns will have been outlawed sometime in the 1980's and by the last decade of the twentieth century long-gun registration will be in effect. Every gun and gun owner, too, will be listed in an instant retrieval central computer. Registration fees will have increased to the point where only the very wealthy will be able to afford to own firearms. An army of federal agents will be confiscating registered rifles and shotguns on trumped-up infractions of dozens of obscure rules. To replace expended shells, hunters and shooters will need to file a comprehensive report stating precisely when and under what conditions the ammunition was used.

Think that last item too pessimistic? It's exactly the situation in Japan today. And bureaucrats in the U.S. are using the "Japan Plan" as a model in plotting firearms control here.

Even more distressing is the thought that those of us who successfully battle the red tape and retain ownership rights to our guns will have few places to use them. In the intervening years, anti-hunters will have succeeded in getting all hunting banned on government lands. And on private lands, agencies such as Occupational Health and Safety Administration (OHSA) will have piled on so many nitpicking regulations under the guise of public safety that landowners will be unable to pay the sky-high liability insurance premiums the regulations will demand. Instead, to protect themselves, they will post their lands against all visitors.

How will all this be brought about?

In the past few years, small groups of obstructionists dedicated to narrow special interests have learned to exploit and subvert a subtle change in the structure of government that has come upon most of us unawares. Basically, the change has switched power from elected representatives to non-elected government employees—the bureaucrats.

Historically, the affairs of the country were directed by explicit, comprehensive laws which had been deliberated, debated and duly passed by elected legislators. But as government became more complex, legislators felt overburdened with technical details and started passing general laws instead. These laws set down policy and describe legislative intent, but leave it up to the bureaucrats to develop, administrate and enforce the rules under which the laws are carried out.

Annually, millions of new administrative rules emanate from hundreds of federal, state and local government agencies. The rules have the force of law and regulate such diverse activities as aspirin advertising, the coloring of oranges, and the waterfowl harvest.

More often than not the rules go far beyond legislative intent, for power has a way of perverting those who wield it into believing that only they know what's good for everybody and that the people are incapable of governing themselves.

A case in point is the Endangered Species Act of 1973. In passing the legislation it was clearly the intent of Congress that the Act was meant to identify and protect major species of animals and birds such as the grizzly bear and the bald eagle. By April 1976 the job appeared to have been completed: 43 species had been identified as endangered and 23 were listed as threatened.

Then, perhaps anticipating job loss, the administrators "reevaluated" the law and determined that it was their duty to extend their powers over all species, including plants and insects. This decision, as one researcher put it, "Is the biggest thing that's happened to taxonomy since Carolus Linnaeus invented the classification system in the 1700's; it will keep us busy for years."

By mid-1978 the number of species on the endangered list had grown to 257 and the list of threatened species had been expanded to 64. The lists include such creatures as the wound fin minnow, hayspring scud and Houston toad. Throughout, no one bothered to ask the fundamental question: "Are we screwing up the natural world by protecting species which nature has destined for extinction because they can't compete for a niche?"

Instead, we took the position that every living thing, no matter how inconsequential, is worthy of man's protection. Generally, the rationale used to espouse this view is the very selfish attitude that "it might prove useful to us someday."

The bureaucrats sat back, nodded, smiled, and went quickly to work formulating rules. Under the new assumptions, their work would never be done.

The above procedure has been aptly summed up in Fri's Law, named after its originator, former Environmental Protection Agency Administrator Robert Fri, which states: "If any agency can regulate, it will."

The various federal agencies publish their administrative rules, proposed and final, weekly in the *Federal Register*. This year, that publication will contain about forty-five-thousand pages. Each of the proposed rules is put into effect after an open period for public comment. Often, this period might be as short as thirty days. Sometimes public hearings are held, usually in some hard-to-find room in the faraway Washington labyrinth.

Since most people haven't the time to study a weekly average of 900 pages of small print to see which rules will affect them, only a limited number of comments are recorded in any single proceeding.

The minority special-interest groups (anti-hunters, anti-trappers, anti-gun groups, and staunch preservationists are masters at this) understand the system and play it like a virtuoso plays a concert violin. They realize, for example, that if several confederates testify during the public input period, and no one files an opposing view, which outdoorsmen seldom do, the bureaucrats in charge will determine that whatever comments received truly reflect the will of the people, thus providing the mandate to put that version in force.

More insidious is that the special interests soon recognize that they can trade on their reputations as anti-establishment activists to garner appointments to policy positions in the bureaucracy. The administration in power, under a rather twisted ideal of "fair play," is generally willing to oblige, seeing these people merely as "private citizens with no vested interest in the outcome."

Nothing could be further from the truth. Once ensconced in a regulatory agency, the bureaucrat has the authority to formulate, approve and enforce the rules and to act as judge and jury for any transgressors. That holds true whether the bureaucrat is at the federal, state, or local level of government.

Some of the new regulations will be right and necessary, of course. We cannot, for example, quarrel with the need to provide funds for waterfowl habitat acquisition and protection through the sale of federal and state waterfowl stamps. Other regulations, however, will be self-serving, meant to expand bureaucratic powers. Still others will be used to promote a favored minority cause while subverting those established programs the bureaucrats and their special-interest accomplices deem less worthy.

As I write this, a movement is underway to controvert legislative intent in the use of Pittman-Robertson and Dingell-Johnson funds. These funds, derived from excise taxes on sporting arms and ammunition and sport fishing equipment, are earmarked for the protection and enhancement of wildlife habitat. Now, some would divert the funds to other uses, one of which is to accelerate the identification and classification of endangered and threatened species. Strangely, proponents of the ploy seem to disregard the connection between the well being of all wildlife and the availability of habitat.

History, however, has never remembered a pessimist. It takes an optimist to effect beneficial change. Optimists, rather than wring their hands and lament "All is lost!" will seek to identify a problem and determine to solve it.

How will outdoorsmen meet the challenge of changing times? One way might be to drop the habit of grousing pessimistically among ourselves at the skeet house, at the ski chalet, at the camper's association annual dinner meeting, and at the conservation club bar. Instead, we must learn to work the bureaucratic system to effect beneficial change, perhaps by using the already well-developed techniques of the anti's. Otherwise, the Outdoor World of January 1, 2000, depicted earlier will come into being by route and will be as hostile as predicted.

New Year's Day this year is not too early to begin.